PRAISE FOR

Reach Out with Acts of Kindness:
A Guide to Helping Others in Crisis

"Tish pours her heart into this informative guide, creating a resource to support anyone in reaching out to those who are struggling with the diverse trials of life. She begins with her own heartbreaking account of the diagnosis, treatment/care, and death of her husband, John—a journey that has not only significantly added to her own life experience with respect to reaching out and receiving support amid life's struggles, but it has also inspired her to author this helpful resource so that others might benefit as well."

—John (Jack) Foley, retired avionics engineer, and deacon

"Letitia E. Hart's *Reach Out with Acts of Kindness: A Guide to Helping Others in Crisis* is a beacon of light in times of darkness. This poignant guide reminds us that compassion and empathy are not just virtues but actionable deeds. Hart beautifully underscores the power of simple gestures and the profound impact they can have on those facing adversity. From the importance of presence to the art of offering support without intrusion, each page resonates with wisdom and warmth. *Reach Out* is not just a book; it's a roadmap to building a community steeped in kindness and understanding. A must-read for anyone looking to make a difference in the lives of others."

—Jay Poling, private wealth financial advisor

"*Reach Out* is a remarkable and much-needed resource for understanding the impact of grief and learning how to support those in crisis. Tish has accomplished something rare. She provides the reader with an opportunity to grieve, process their trauma alongside her, and then shift into healing and growth. This allows us to lay down social defenses so we can consider the needs of others. This book truly is a call to action. The mystery has been removed. We are now equipped to care for others. Her passion to help is evident, and I will be recommending *Reach Out* on an ongoing basis!"

—Paula Allocca PhD, PMHNP-BC

"Tish Hart's exceptionally well-written, deeply personal journey helps to remind us of how precious life is, how resilient we are, and the importance of honoring others. The in-depth advice she shares to help support someone navigating a sudden life-altering traumatic event is perfectly timed in the post-COVID era. Personally, having a mother and partner with life-altering illnesses, I could relate to Tish's story so deeply. *Reach Out* is an invaluable resource to remind us we can find easy ways to lift up others, be understanding, and be thoughtful. Tish reminds us it is not about finding the perfect words to say; it is about treating others as humans. I will keep *Reach Out* on hand for creative and simple ideas to connect with others respectfully."

—Sarah M Dowdy, DDS

"*Reach Out with Acts of Kindness: A Guide to Helping Others in Crisis* is an excellent read for those looking to find ways to lend a hand to family or friends going through tough times. It is written with a warm, personal touch that pulls you in from the very beginning. It is filled with practical advice that you can easily use in your life when needed."

—Alison E. Alford, MD, FAHS, FAAN

"Many of us know through painful personal experience how hard it is to reorient our lives in the aftermath of some kind of unexpected crisis or loss. Many of us have also felt helpless while watching a friend, family member, or neighbor go through a difficult and disorienting experience. This book is a rare but much-needed resource: a combination of heartfelt personal reflection and practical advice for those who are either navigating a crisis or who are eager to help someone else find their way through one of life's many storms. It is a treasure trove of hard-won wisdom and an inspiring and humbling reminder that there is often much more that we can do than we may realize—if we but have the courage and compassion to reach out."

—Rev. Andrew P. Whitehead, pastor and head of staff

"Discover the extraordinary journey within the pages of *Reach Out with Acts of Kindness* by Letitia Hart. In this remarkable guide, Letitia Hart fearlessly charts a course through life's intricate maze of challenges. Drawing from her own poignant experiences—where tragedy and grief intersect—she sets a high watermark for readers to measure their own struggles against. This isn't just a narrative; it's a beacon of wisdom. Hart's words resonate with insight and relatability, illuminating the path toward supporting others during their darkest hours. Whether you're navigating someone else's storm or weathering your own tempest, her counsel is a lifeline. As we confront life's unyielding realities—often as unforgiving as they are inevitable—Hart implores us to cultivate an ethos of empathy. It's the difference between merely surviving heartbreak and triumphantly crossing our own bridges of pain. *Reach Out with Acts of Kindness* reminds us that kindness isn't a luxury; it's a universal currency. And in times of need, we all possess the power to make a difference."

—Adam J. Thompson, author of *Hard to Keep Happy*.

"Every human being is exposed to the indiscriminate and universal concepts of grief, adversity, struggle, or hard times. Yet, how we love and support one another during these tumultuous life moments leaves a lot to be desired. Thankfully, Letitia Hart selflessly shares not only her own personal story but also provides a guidebook for how to help others undergoing a crisis. There's no longer an excuse for not showing up for another in distress or pain."

—Stephen Panus, author of *Walk On* and motivational speaker

"*Reach Out with Acts of Kindness* gives the author's firsthand account of living through tragedy. After detailing her own experience with her husband's illness and death, Letitia Hart provides a simple and practical list of ways to help someone in crisis. Letitia reminds readers of some things most of us know but often fail to implement. Kindness and compassion need to be more than mere expressions of 'thoughts and prayers'; they need to be followed up with actual deeds. Unless put into action, our good intentions are meaningless. It's in the doing that we truly offer our support and our love to those who are hurting."

> —Jennifer E. Hassel, author of *Badass Grief: Changing Gears, Moving Forward*

Reach Out with Acts of Kindness:
A Guide to Helping Others in Crisis

by Letitia (Tish) E. Hart

© Copyright 2024 Letitia E. Hart

ISBN 979-8-88824-294-0

All rights reserved. No part of this publication may be reproduced, stored in a retrieval system, or transmitted in any form or by any means—electronic, mechanical, photocopy, recording, or any other—except for brief quotations in printed reviews, without the prior written permission of the author.

Published by

köehlerbooks™

3705 Shore Drive
Virginia Beach, VA 23455
800-435-4811
www.koehlerbooks.com

Reach Out
with Acts of
Kindness

A Guide to Helping Others in Crisis

Letitia E. Hart

VIRGINIA BEACH
CAPE CHARLES

Dedicated to John—
husband, partner, and best friend—
you will always be in my heart.

Table of Contents

Prologue 1
Introduction 5

PART 1 7
   My Story 8

PART 2 63
   Afterthoughts 64

PART 3 89
   Helping Others in Crisis 90
   Understanding Emotions 94
      Empathy and Compassion 94
      Be Sensitive 95
      A Pass 98
      When Privacy Is Requested 98
      The Gift of Time 99
   Helpful Suggestions of Support 100
      Keeping Everyone Informed 100
      Cards! Cards! Cards! 101
      Pick Up the Phone 102
      Providing Meals 103
      Fill the Freezer 108
      Food Items 109
      Gift Cards 109
      Flowers, Gifts, Treats, etc. 110
      Offer to Run Errands, Complete Tasks, or Handle Routine Responsibilities 111
      Child Care/Pet Care 112
      Offer to Accompany Someone to Doctor's Appointments and/or Treatments 112

Offer to Sit with Someone Who May Be Homebound
or Ill...113
Offer to Accompany Someone to a Funeral Home,
Cemetery, or House of Worship.................................113
Coworkers, Neighbors, Acquaintances......................114
People in Crisis Living in an Apartment
or Condominium...114
Suggestions to Lend Support for Those Living Out
of Town..115
Hospital, Rehabilitation/Treatment Facility, and
Home Visits...115
Children Encountering a Troubling Period...............117
Young Families Enduring a Troubling Time.............118
Fundraisers..119
Common Struggles and Troublesome Times................120
Crumbling Relationships, Separation, Divorce.........120
Job Loss..121
Financial Strains...121
First-Time Parents or Family Additions....................122
Minor Struggles..122
Other Difficult Situations..123
Rehabilitation Facilities...124
Assisted Living, Nursing Home,
Health-Care Facility, or the Homebound..................124
Pregnancy Complications/Miscarriage......................125
Tragic/Horrific Ordeals..126
Hospice...127
Home Emergencies...127
Natural Disasters..128
Additional Thoughts..129
Ask..129
Medical Equipment or Essential Items......................130
Listen..130

    Caregivers..131
    Remember Other Family Members.................................132
    Reach Out—Be Creative..133
    More Ways to Reach Out..133
    Gift Bags/Gift Baskets..134
    Chemotherapy or Other Medical Treatments................135
When the Waves of Emotions Continue................................136
    Just Because..136
    Sensitive Dates and Holidays...138
    Show Up. Be There. Be Present.....................................138
    Just Do...139
    Do the Unexpected...139
    Acknowledgment..140
    Prayers..141
Keep In Mind...142
    Step Outside of Yourself; It's Not About You................142
    What Is Your Gift?..143
What NOT To Say or Do When
Someone is Going Through a Crisis.......................................144

PART 4...**155**
Helping Others Following a Crisis..156
The Darkness of Death..158
    Death..158
    Death of a Child..159
    Death by Suicide...159
Understanding Emotions and Ways to Offer Support
Following a Tragic Period..160
    Be Sensitive...160
    Providing Meals/Food..162
    Funeral Home Visitations, Memorial Services, and
    Celebrations of Life..165
    Guest Book..166

- Wordage—Loss, Passed, Death 166
- Wordage—Sorry 167
- What to Say Following a Traumatic Ordeal or Death 167
- Sympathy Cards 168
- Memorial Funds 170
- Children, Teens, or Young Adults Coping with Loss 170
- The Time Immediately Following a Difficult Ordeal or Death 171
- Crisis or Grief Assistance/Counseling 171

Additional Suggestions 173
- More Thoughtful Ways to Lend Support 173
- Pick Up the Phone 174
- Invitations 174
- Inclusion 175

When the Waves of Emotions Continue 176
- Sensitive Dates and Holidays 176
- Individuals Having Gone Through or Completed a Recovery Program 177
- Show Up, Be There, Be Present, and Most Importantly, Listen 177
- Just Do 178
- Lift Up 178
- Acknowledgment 179

Keep In Mind 180
- It's Not About You 180
- What Is Your Gift? 181

What NOT to Say or Do Following a Crisis 182

Quick Guide on Ways to Reach Out **199**
Important Takeaways **201**
Acknowledgements **202**
Bibliography **204**

Prologue

About twenty years ago, a dear friend received devastating news no one is ever prepared to hear: she had cancer. After enduring several years of grueling treatments and countless hospitalizations, my friend passed away two years after her initial diagnosis. During her major health crisis, I searched for ways to offer comfort and support to her and her family, but I could not find suitable material or resources that provided useful information and spoke to me, especially since she lived in another state.

In early June 2015, my husband, John, was diagnosed with brain cancer. We felt like we were sucker punched into a nightmare we never expected to experience. Out of nowhere, we were plunged into an ominous medical crisis, without a detailed map to help us navigate the thrashing waters of the unforeseen tempestuous sea of uncertainties and countless worries. We never saw the blinding flashing warning signs of brain cancer. Over the next heartbreaking, gut-wrenching, stressful, and challenging six months that ultimately ended in John's death, my family and I encountered a roller coaster of unsettling emotional and physical highs and lows. The outpouring of heartfelt support we received during this troublesome time, emotionally and hands-on, was immeasurable and truly gave us the strength to get through many days.

At some point in life, everyone will face a battle, tragedy, or life-altering event, unexpected or possibly anticipated, whether it is a health issue, addiction, emotional or physical abuse, depression, mental illness, drug overdose, move to a health-care facility, crumbling relationship, separation, divorce, suicide, death, job loss, financial strains, home emergencies, natural disasters, etc. Everyone has a story and personal journey. Many books are readily available that focus on these issues, but few are centered on concrete ways for outsiders to lend comfort and backing to those struggling during and following a crisis or death.

This guide presents simple, relatable approaches to help those enduring any type of hardship. After experiencing a devastating time and talking with others who have gone through similar situations or difficult adversities, this book also highlights the many wavering emotions and challenges those in crisis may encounter with clear-cut practical tips, thoughts, insights, and guidance on how to reach out and respond during the troubling time and in the aftermath.

In early 2020, the world experienced the coronavirus, a massive-scale health pandemic affecting many individuals, families, businesses, and governments. The disaster resulted in emotional, financial, and life-changing uncertainties for everyone. This resource provides helpful ideas as traces of the virus and the repercussions continue to linger.

I truly felt called to write this book; I could not not write this guide. I am an average person who never expected to experience tragedy. Reaching out to others is a topic I have always been passionate about, regardless of the hardship or predicament. Although I have no medical, psychiatric, or psychological education, I have learned a lot about people, relationships, and life, as well as myself, in the six months John was ill and following his death. After living through a heartbreaking period, I have a lot to share to help those in crisis, and I am fueled by reaching out to others when they need it the most.

It is not my intention for this book to be about me. I begin these pages with my story, to help readers understand the struggles, difficulties, and heartaches my family endured after my husband's sudden fatal health diagnosis, but you may skip to the third part of the book, "How to Help Others in Crisis," for suggestions on how to aid those dealing with a tumultuous situation.

Prologue

Several friends have asked me if writing this guide was a therapeutic endeavor. I can answer the question with a firm *no*. There is nothing healing or positive when reliving a devastating time. I hope to turn the tragic period we went through into something beneficial for others dealing with hardship. There is a clear lack of accessible resources in this area. This guide is a valuable initiative for outsiders who want to lend assistance but may be unsure or hesitant about how to proceed. I know others cared about my family and me during our tragic time, but I later became aware that many struggled with how to help us during the darkest period in our lives, and even now, many years later.

I am truly blessed to have had the support of my son, Daniel, daughter and son-in-law, Alyssa and Kevin, and several family members and friends who stood by me, held my hand, and provided an essential safety net of support during the lowest and most fearful period I have ever experienced. With the love, prayers, care, and backing that were bestowed upon me, I vowed to reach out and pay it forward.

Introduction

At some point in life, everyone will face a perplexing roadblock or battle or be touched by someone experiencing a challenging period. Some people will be fortunate to live a long life with only a few minor obstacles or difficulties, while others will endure crisis after crisis. It is a given that no one is immune to struggles. Everyone has a story, a personal journey.

The coronavirus pandemic, which became apparent in the United States in mid-March 2020, was a major health catastrophe that affected everyone. This unanticipated crisis may have added a heightened, painful layer for those already wrestling with a traumatic situation. People experienced social distancing, inconvenient shortages of items at the grocery store, losing a loved one or friend to the virus, daily life struggles, unforeseen financial strains, work layoffs, job losses, uncertainties of local, state, and worldwide businesses, and questionable futures.

There are no guarantees in life. Situations, circumstances, setbacks, and everyday life can shift or change in a split second, altering a planned path. We all face the same day-to-day routines and demands while attempting to live each day to the fullest. When tragedy strikes, aren't we called to try to lessen another's heartaches and burdens by reaching out? Those who are stumbling in life or facing trying circumstances may be aching for guidance or silently crying out for help, yet they may feel hesitant, uneasy, or unsure how to ask for assistance, support, or direction. Outsiders are often unaware of the challenges others may be up against.

Difficult times are when family and friends are needed the most.

Tragic events put everyday life into a straightforward perspective. Our time in the here and now is short and precious. No one should ever feel alone, fall through the cracks, or be forgotten when facing a difficult time. I repeat this many times throughout the book because it is so important. No one should suffer in silence.

Life is busy, life is complicated, and life can be hard, but what are we all here for? Reaching out to those in need and offering comfort and support is what life is all about—in good times and bad, regardless of the circumstances. No one truly knows what someone may be going through or has faced. Everyone deals with a crisis and its aftermath differently.

My goal is for readers to take away the importance of family, friends, and acquaintances and reach out to those suffering with empathy, compassion, and simple acts of kindness. This resource is a call to action. Step outside of yourself. Do not be a bystander on life's sidewalk, aware of others standing in the middle of the street in hardship. Open your heart to those hurting.

Reach out.

PART 1

My Story

June 2, 2015 ... John and I looked at each other in total shock, and we knew our lives would never be the same.

May 2015

On a Thursday afternoon in late May, John met me at the door after work and asked me to go straight to the back deck. He had prepared a happy hour with a nice chilled bottle of chardonnay and our favorite cheeses and crackers. It was a beautiful, warm, sunny afternoon, and John proposed we relax and take advantage of the gorgeous weather. At this point in time, we were sailing through life on calm seas, trying to slow down, enjoy every moment, and soak up all the wonderful things in life. I got comfortable in a chair on the deck as John attempted to pour me a glass of wine. I noticed he was having trouble aligning the bottle over the wine glass. I nonchalantly joked that I was *really* thirsty, so could he hurry up and fill my glass? He laughed and said his right arm felt *clumsy*, and he proceeded to pour me a glass using his left arm even though he was right-handed. This was unusual, and I casually remarked that he should keep an eye on his right arm, and if there was no improvement by Monday morning, he needed to get it checked out by his primary care physician. Little did we realize, this was the beginning of an unimaginable nightmare. We enjoyed the happy hour and the delightful, warm May afternoon and shared our day, oblivious of what was to come.

Friday seemed like any other, with John working in his home

office while I checked off items on my to-do list. Friends were hosting a shower on Saturday afternoon for our daughter, Alyssa, who was expecting her first baby in early July. John and I planned a dinner party that evening to spend more time with local friends and out-of-town guests. I spent most of Friday prepping for Saturday night's gathering. The baby shower was wonderful. Alyssa and I felt blessed to enjoy the afternoon with family and dear friends, and John and I looked forward to the arrival of our first grandchild. I did not give any more thought to John's right arm, nor did he mention any clumsiness that morning or afternoon. During dinner Saturday night, John indifferently commented that he was still having trouble using his right hand and arm and ate his meal with his left, which was not an easy task. Again, we did not think too much of it.

On Sunday evening, we had friends over for a cookout, and John mentioned his continued mobility issues. He used his left arm to grill and eat his meal, and we had a nice evening catching up with friends. After tidying up, I reminded John to call his doctor first thing Monday morning to schedule an appointment. John thought he may have pulled a muscle in his neck that affected his right arm. We also discussed the possibility of a mild stroke, but honestly, we weren't too concerned since he had no other symptoms and was in good health.

I was slightly miffed when I came home on Monday afternoon to learn that John had not seen his doctor, but he had made an appointment for the next day. I had something scheduled at the same time, but a gut feeling tugged at me that I needed to accompany him, so I canceled my plans. I wanted to be sure John's symptoms were fully conveyed to his physician.

June 2, 2015

Ten minutes after listening to what had been going on for the past five days, John's primary physician called the nearest hospital's emergency room to alert them we were coming. He did not feel an ambulance was necessary but suspected John suffered a mild stroke. Further tests were needed to find out what was going on. We calmly drove to the ER, got John checked in, and patiently waited for the exams.

Several routine tests were conducted, but nothing out of the ordinary was detected. John was a healthy sixty-one-year-old man; he was trim, exercised regularly, and ate a healthy, well-balanced diet, so we were puzzled. When the initial assessments were negative, John was admitted for additional examinations. Once he was assigned a room, an MRI of his head was ordered. Like many people, John was never a fan of hospitals and, quite frankly, any medical tests, so I was concerned about him undergoing the procedure. Surprisingly, he did not experience any issues with the MRI.

Later that day, a neurosurgeon came to John's hospital room and delivered the devastating news. The MRI revealed that John had tumors growing in his brain. He had brain cancer. John had a tumor the size of a baby carrot on the lower left side of the brainstem and a smaller tumor on the upper right side of his brain. The neurosurgeon said these locations were the worst places for tumors (especially the large one), and due to the locations, they were inoperable. Called glioblastomas (GBMs), this cancer is completely random and typically occurs in men aged fifty to seventy, although GBMs also occur in women. There is no rhyme or reason why John developed these tumors; it just happened. Thankfully, GBMs are not genetic, so our children need not worry. The neurosurgeon reported the large tumor had probably been growing for six to nine months; it was only a week earlier that a sign of the tumors, the clumsiness, disclosed itself. John and I looked at each other in total shock, and we knew our lives would never be the same.

The neurosurgeon reviewed the report with me, and I was completely startled by the large size of the main tumor. John never looked at the image; I am not sure why. Maybe disbelief? He was stunned by the diagnosis and only remarked that he could not believe tumors were growing inside his head. Never in a million years did John or I ever expect to receive this kind of news—brain cancer. We were totally unprepared to hear this report. The reality of what we were up against was unfathomable and out of our control. We felt like we had been blindsided into a nightmare of incredulity. Less than a week earlier, we were in a serene spot in life, enjoying a cocktail hour. We were no longer sailing on calm seas. Under dark, threatening skies, out of nowhere, we lost all navigational routes. This was a dire disturbance we were not ready to go through. We had no choice but to do whatever was necessary to attempt to weather this unwanted, unpredictable, uncharted squall.

A biopsy would determine the exact type of cancer John had so appropriate treatment options could be considered. Even though the neurosurgeon was certain the tumors were GBMs, John could not receive any form of treatment unless a biopsy positively confirmed it. Unfortunately, the biopsy would be extremely dangerous and possibly life-threatening. The only way to get to the large tumor was from the top of John's head, down about five or six inches; the second tumor was too small to obtain a biopsy. We were told the procedure could result in 1) permanent paralysis as a portion of the brain could accidentally be touched, and/or 2) bleeding out on the operating table, and/or 3) death. Due to the risky nature of the biopsy, an MRI of John's trunk area was recommended. If tumors were found in that region, a biopsy would be easier and safer than going into the brain, and it would be sufficient to determine the type of cancer so proper treatment could be thought out. Unfortunately, John's trunk area was clean as a whistle, so the dicey procedure into his brain was the only option. The biopsy was scheduled for the following Monday afternoon.

Alyssa and her husband, Kevin, met us at the hospital and learned the grim news. At eight months pregnant, Alyssa's health worried me. I feared this heartbreaking development could endanger her pregnancy. Our son, Daniel, was finishing college out west. We did not share the seriousness of the diagnosis. We wanted him to focus on his classes to graduate in August.

John was discharged from the hospital that Thursday afternoon, and it was recommended that we get our ducks in a row before the biopsy procedure on Monday. Despite the devastating report of brain cancer, John and I remained upbeat and knew we needed to get our lives and paperwork in order. I took notes of all the information John thought I needed to know. We went over passwords to various accounts, where he kept certain documents, who I needed to contact for his businesses, how I should handle various personal and work issues, what was in our safe deposit boxes, what type of funeral he wanted, etc., etc., etc. John and I were so distraught by the report of brain cancer that we truly could not fully digest the tragic news. John sent out a mass email to family, friends, and business associates, sharing the shocking, unfortunate diagnosis.

We remained positive through the weekend, but of course, all John and I talked about was the bleak finding. This development had caught us completely off guard. John said many times throughout the weekend, "I can't believe I have cancerous tumors growing inside my head." John recalled meeting with Kevin the week prior to go over business matters. John was having trouble writing, and Kevin suggested he see his doctor if the messy penmanship continued. Neither John nor Kevin shared this concern with me at the time. John also mentioned that he tripped on a sidewalk the previous week. Sidewalks in the city are often uneven, but John said that he knew the section well and always watched out for it, making his stumble out of the ordinary. We recognized that these mishaps were likely early signs of the insidious tumors.

Over the weekend, the notes on my legal pad continued to grow. I would think of important questions to ask John, or he would mention something essential I needed to know.

At one point, we couldn't find the keys to one of our cars that had been serviced that week. John insisted he gave them to me, but I was adamant that he had not. After searching and retracing our steps, we realized locating the keys was the least of our worries. We spent the remainder of the weekend trying not to dwell on the shocking diagnosis, yet it was hard not to drown in the endless uncertainties and angst. Friends came over for dinner on Sunday, which was a nice distraction from the risky biopsy weighing heavily on our minds.

June 8, 2015

Monday arrived, and the morning was hauntingly quiet, slow, and uneasy. As we got in the car to head to the hospital, I rummaged through my purse for something, and alas ... there were the missing car keys! John gave me a *look* and said, "I told you I gave you the keys! I am going to ask the doctor if he will do a 'twofer' as you apparently need brain surgery, too, since you did not remember that I gave you the keys!" His comments lightened our moods, and we could not stop laughing.

Alyssa and Kevin met us at the hospital that afternoon. I was able to accompany John to the pre-op area for about ten minutes before he was prepped for surgery. He and I tearfully said what might have been our final goodbyes. Not knowing if John would be permanently paralyzed or make it through the procedure, it was a heartbreaking, sorrowful, private occasion that I will never forget. It was a Kodak moment, a very bad Kodak moment. I was truly scared, and even though John did not say or show it, I knew he was as well.

It was an extremely unnerving and long afternoon. As Alyssa, Kevin, and I restlessly sat in the waiting room, a friend unexpectedly appeared with cold drinks, snacks, magazines, and, most importantly, support. I could not believe she found us. I would have had no idea how to find the family of a patient undergoing surgery. She sat with us for about half an hour as we nervously waited for the biopsy to be over; her visit helped get our minds off the jarring ticking clock.

Following the surgery and post-op recovery, John was moved

to the ICU. The neurosurgeon reported that the procedure went very well, and we would be able to see him later that evening. I was cautiously relieved. When Alyssa, Kevin, and I were finally able to see John, he was awake and alert and said he could not believe he was alive. He knew who he was, who we were, where he was, and why he was there. The unsettling storm clouds opened for a bit, but I knew we were drifting in an unfamiliar, ominous direction. John remained overnight in the ICU for observation. At 9:30 that night, Alyssa, Kevin, and I returned home to a cooler filled with a delicious quiche, fresh fruit, and a dessert our friend from the hospital had dropped off. We were all emotionally exhausted and very hungry. The late-night dinner was so appreciated.

The next day, John and I met with the neurosurgeon and oncologist on staff at the hospital. John showed no signs of paralysis or other troubling issues. We learned that the left side of the brain, where the large tumor was, controls the right side of the body. The large tumor was growing and touching the part of the brain that controlled the right side of John's body, resulting in the clumsiness of his right hand and arm. The biopsy confirmed the tumors were GBMs.

The oncologist explained that GBMs are an extremely aggressive malignancy, and standard treatment is chemotherapy and radiation simultaneously. Because of this ugly, scheming cancer, time was of the essence. If John did not receive treatment soon, he would most likely only live about four more weeks. There are no words to describe how we felt. Many people with GBMs live about twelve to fifteen months after the tumor starts growing. For John, that was most likely six to nine months prior to us noticing his clumsiness. The initial shock of brain cancer clouded my thinking. I had a hard time grasping the prognosis and timeline. However, everyone's case is different. There is no definitive time frame for living with GBMs. When I asked the oncologist for his professional opinion on trials, he adamantly said if John was a candidate for *any* type of trial, he should definitely be a part of one. This was a huge red flag to me.

The cancer was serious. Deep down, I knew that John's diagnosis was most likely a death sentence.

A staff member and the hospital chaplain stopped by John's ICU room to lend emotional support and go over his medical directive, power of attorney, will, funeral considerations, etc. John and I had discussed our end-of-life wishes in the past, so we were comfortable having these discussions with the hospital team. Alyssa was in the room, taken aback by the inappropriate timing of these talks. I explained that everyone should discuss final intentions and arrangements, even if it's uncomfortable; no one should wait until a tragedy occurs to have these conversations.

John could not believe he was alive and continued to show no signs of paralysis or other problems following the biopsy procedure. His only hopes were to see our first grandchild, who was due in early July, know that Daniel graduated college in August, and be able to celebrate his sixty-second birthday in early September. Despite the troubling report, John remained positive and hopeful. He had no regrets in life, he said, but over the years, he was disappointed in several people. I believe our minds are full of expectations and disillusioned circumstances, and when those assumptions fall short, letdowns set in. John shared his disappointments with me, which will remain private out of respect to him. When death looks you directly in the eye, you cannot help but see your entire life flash before you in an instant, and I think this was the case with John. It was comforting and serene to hear John say he had no regrets in life, as death was looming. Alyssa, Kevin, and I were eager to bring him home that evening, where I began the agonizing search for any trials to extend John's life and beat the odds of this aggressive, fatal cancer.

The next day, John apologized for what this diagnosis meant for our lives. He knew we had an agonizing, fearful time ahead of us; this was just the beginning of a violent, wavering storm. "I'm so sorry to do this to you," he said. I replied, "It's okay. It could have been me, and we will get through this together." I meant what I said from the bottom of my heart. I was going to be right by John's side during this heartbreaking time, no matter what challenges or obstacles came into play. John and I never discussed our bleak situation again. Although our lives were totally off course and out of our control, we stuck together and continued to forge ahead.

As much as we downplayed the diagnosis of John's brain cancer, Daniel got permission from his professors to miss several classes and flew home to see his dad in person. Daniel realized the gravity of the discovery. It took everything to convince him to return to college to finish his last few classes to graduate in August. In fact, I had to guilt Daniel into it by blaming John. I said, "Your *dad* and I would be very upset if you do not go back and complete your classes. There is nothing you can do here right now anyway." Daniel reluctantly returned to college, and I can only imagine how hard it was for him to stay focused on his studies. We kept him apprised of appointments and possible treatment options.

Mid-June 2015

I did not know anything about this type of brain cancer, and frankly, I had never heard of GBMs. I had to swiftly educate myself on this deadly disease. I began the laborious search for trials to hopefully beat this conniving cancer—or at least defend the growing tumors. It was an overwhelming and exhausting quest that I blindly delved into alone. John was recovering from the biopsy surgery and was not able to study or research this cancer or possible trials. The hours and days I spent looking into current and future studies, trials, experimental options, and treatments were long and bewildering. I felt like an unschooled acrobat on a precarious tightrope of unsureness, bracing for upcoming missteps.

A few weeks after the biopsy, John had trouble walking, and the neurosurgeon put in an order for physical and occupational therapy at home to improve his mobility and maintain his strength. The large tumor was pushing on the part of the brain that controlled not only John's right hand and arm but also his right leg. The physical therapist came to our home several days a week and worked to strengthen his right side and teach him how to walk safely with his gimpy right leg. He stumbled on a regular basis when walking; his toes caught the floor and made him trip. John's right arm became useless and easily came out of the socket. I was shown how to put his lifeless arm back in the socket, and John was given a sling to hold it in place.

I mentioned to a friend that John was having trouble walking, and she offered up her mother's transport chair, which is a lightweight, step-down wheelchair. My friend's mother had used it for many years before she passed away. She called it Redd Rooster, as it was red in color, and Redd was her mother's last name. I was so grateful to borrow Redd Rooster, which John and I renamed *Big Red*. It was a blessing to have the chair, and I could not thank my friend enough for letting us borrow it. Thankfully, John was okay with using Big Red.

The minute John was diagnosed with brain cancer, he was no longer able to drive, which, of course, he was not pleased to hear. As each day passed, getting John in and out of the house and in and out of the car continued to be physically challenging. John had lost complete use of his right arm, right hand, and right leg due to the tumors affecting his movements. Aware of the difficulties John and I were encountering, the neurosurgeon put in an order for a handicap placard. The placard arrived in the mail about ten days after I sent in the required paperwork, and it made it easier to take John out as I could take advantage of handicap parking spaces. John had several friends offer to pick him up and take him to various gatherings, which was very kind and thoughtful, but I felt extremely uneasy letting someone else shoulder this responsibility. If John fell or experienced an unexpected issue, I wanted it to be on my watch and not someone else's.

The occupational therapist came to the house once a week for a few weeks. On her first visit, she looked for safety risks and advised me to pick up several rugs that were potential tripping hazards. I was given many helpful tips on easy ways to help John bathe, dress, and feed himself. The therapist suggested I get someone out to the house to install handicap bars by the toilets and in the showers. I thought, *Who do I even contact to have handicap bars installed*? A deluge of emotions flooded my mind about John's diagnosis and all the things I needed to accomplish in a day, from researching trials and handicap bars to keeping up with John's business, our personal business, numerous phone calls, emails, and daily mail while simultaneously wondering what unexpected thing would pop up next on my already full plate.

It wasn't long before John needed my assistance to safely get up and out of a chair and return to a seated position; walking alone was out of the question. To get from point A to point B, he would stand behind me and hold onto my shoulder with his left hand to steady himself, and he would shadow me, shuffling like a slow-moving choo choo train departing the station. Stairs were extremely challenging and dangerous. The physical therapist showed us how John should safely climb and descend stairs, yet I cringed with each step, hoping he would not fall. If he happened to take a spill, I prayed he would not take me down with him. I was stunned how quickly his right arm and hand became totally useless and walking alone was out of the question.

The physical therapist continued to come to the house twice a week, and John was given a gait belt so I could steady him when he walked/shuffled or grab him if he started to fall. A special walker was ordered for John, which we named *Steady Eddy*, suitable for his physical limitations. (Don't ask me why we named inanimate objects like Big Red and Steady Eddy; we just did.) John was taught how to utilize Steady Eddy when getting in and out of a chair and how to safely walk with it. Since walking was more challenging, the physical therapist put in an order for John to be fitted for a brace on his right foot/leg at a local prosthetic office to deal with the tripping issues.

Steady Eddy quickly became essential daily equipment. John used Steady Eddy when he got up from a chair and back down to a seated position and to brace himself when walking, with me, of course, overseeing his safety. At times, Steady Eddy made it difficult to maneuver around objects and enter and exit some offices, buildings, restaurants, etc. John held Steady Eddy as I pushed him in Big Red through the house, office building doorways, hallways, elevators, or wherever we were going. At times, Steady Eddy's legs got hung up on a doorframe or knocked into something as we passed by. Of course, I was not to blame as Big Red's chauffeur nor John as Steady Eddy's keeper. We could only laugh at our quandary, blaming any mishaps on these medical equipment devices.

The first visit to the prosthetic office was eye-opening. Now that we had the handicap placard, I could take advantage of a parking space close to the entryway. I got Big Red and Steady Eddy out of the car and helped John into Big Red while he held Steady Eddy. I was surprised to find one single door leading to a small public lobby; a few feet inside, there was another single door that opened to a hallway to various businesses and medical offices. I consider myself a wheelchair pro. I had a lot of experience when my dad required one, but the two single doors close together were nearly impossible to manage by myself. I had to hold the first door open with my left arm while backing in Big Red. Thankfully, a gentleman exiting the building held the second door open for us, and John and I proceeded to the prosthetic office.

Once we checked in, John was taken to a private examination room where his right leg and foot were wrapped with plastic wrap, and a quick-drying putty-type substance was applied. When hardened, the putty material turned into a stiff plastic brace. The brace would be flat on the bottom and fit the outline of John's right foot with Velcro straps around his calf to hold it in place. The intended result was to keep John's right foot secure, preventing his toes from bending to avoid tripping. It would take a little over a week for the brace to be made. The technician suggested we bring the shoes John would be wearing daily when we returned for the final fitting. We were told to get a size larger shoe for his right foot to accommodate the brace.

I had absolutely no idea what kind of shoes to get, but I knew they needed to be easy to slip on and off. An open Velcro-type sandal was suggested by the technician, and I thought I should probably get two pairs of footwear, one pair in size nine and one pair in size ten. After discussing this dilemma with John, he said, "Just go to the shoe store and tell them you need one size nine sandal for a left foot and one size ten sandal for a right foot." I thought, *What? A shoe store is not going to sell me sandals in different sizes.* I found a nice pair of Velcro sandals and bought two pairs, one in each size. We made it work.

Ten days after John's right foot and leg were cast for the brace, we returned for the final fitting. I parked in a handicapped spot, got Big Red and Steady Eddy from the trunk, and helped John into Big Red with him holding Steady Eddy, our regular routine. Unfortunately, no one could lend assistance through the double doors, so I maneuvered through by myself. It was a huge struggle getting Big Red through the doorways and into the medical office, but I did it. Of course, Steady Eddy knocked into the doorframes and other stationary building objects as we passed by. I was completely worn out and mentioned to the receptionist how difficult it was to get a person in a wheelchair into this office . . . a prosthetic office! I thought, *What the hell is this irony?* I consider myself somewhat young and in shape and could not fathom someone fifteen or twenty years older dealing with this. The receptionist said the building accessibility fell to the owner of the office complex. Yes, the building was handicap suitable; however, in my opinion, it was negligent for anyone with a handicap. A push-button door-opening device would have made entering and exiting the building much easier for those with a wheelchair, crutches, a walker, etc.

We left the prosthetic office with him wearing two different sizes of sandals to accommodate the brace. Once again, I had the pleasure of fighting the two single doors as we exited the building. I now understand—from a caretaking perspective—some of the everyday struggles anyone with a handicap may encounter.

On June 30, a phone call at 1:30 a.m. woke us up. Alyssa was having labor pains. She called again later in the morning and suggested we get to the hospital by noon. Mid-morning, I got John, Big Red, and Steady Eddy into the car, and we headed to the hospital to await the baby news. Our grandson, Wyatt, was born that afternoon, and what a true blessing and joy it was to welcome this new ray of sunshine!

July 2015

John had been a voracious reader since elementary school and was always reading several books at a time. On many occasions since his diagnosis in early June, John would be in the living room, sitting in a chair, not reading, not watching TV, not doing anything, just sitting. I would say, "Why don't I get one of your books, and you can catch up on your reading?" His reply was always, "No, that's okay. I'm fine." This went on for weeks. I did not think too much into it at the time, but looking back, his idleness was a sign that something was not right.

While John sat quietly in the living room, I would sometimes be on the computer in a nearby space researching GBMs, trials, and treatments, as well as keeping up with daily emails or other communications, and I could look around the corner to check on him. One afternoon, I peeked into the living room and saw that John had slipped off his chair to the floor. I ran into the room and tried to get him back into the chair, but he was deadweight and unable to help himself get up. I called a neighbor who quickly came over, and we were able to get John back into the chair.

The stress, anxiety, and worry of what John and I were up against were unbearable, yet we had no choice but to push forward to find a study or treatment. The fear and uncertainty robbed what little hope I had as each day passed. Since John was not able to research trials, this responsibility weighed solely on my shoulders. I was optimistic when I found a trial at Duke University, showing positive signs in treating GBMs. When I told John about it, he said, "I always wanted to say I went to Duke." I could not help but laugh at his tongue-in-cheek comment. John always had a good sense of humor and a fun-loving personality, which continued even during dark times.

I reviewed and filled out the extensive trial application to enroll John in this study. Biopsy slides needed to be forwarded to Duke to accompany the paperwork. There was no resource to guide me through acquiring the slides, so I made numerous calls to various medical departments at the local hospital until I eventually spoke with someone in the correct area and relayed the address where the slides needed to be sent. This was a mind-boggling learning experience and one I wish I did not have to undergo. I spent countless hours completing umpteen forms, copying, and overnighting various documents, sometimes late at night, while caring for John. The angst and anxiety stole what little strength and faith I had and prayed for.

Once Duke received the completed forms, required medical documents, and biopsy slides, we had to wait several days to learn if John would be accepted into this trial. During this time, I did additional research on the study, looking into where we might stay while at Duke for appointments and treatments, etc. Our hopes were quickly squashed when I received a call from the head doctor overseeing the trial. He informed me that John could not be a participant. John had two tumors (the baby carrot-size one and the smaller one), and the protocol for the experimental program only allowed for one growth. Our anticipated prayers immediately plummeted. We were barely treading water, our life vests out of reach as we struggled through rough, choppy seas.

Nevertheless, I found another trial that was showing favorable signs of treating GBMs or possibly keeping tumors at bay. If accepted into this local program, John would be in the second study group. The paperwork involved was lengthy and gnarly, and I thoroughly read the detailed documents multiple times from the first page to the end, jotting down questions or concerns. With any trial, side effects are likely, but they can be worth the risk if life could be extended. By the time I was ready to sign the paperwork, the head radiologist called to report that John was not a candidate for the study. His MRI revealed that 15 percent of the main tumor was in the brainstem, which did not meet the program's protocol. We were devastated—once again. I now have a better understanding of trials and how programs must adhere to the set requirements and protocols to keep the study on point. The rough current seemed to be pushing us further and further into a dark, ever-changing, violent sea of quandary.

John and I promptly met with the oncologist overseeing the area trial, who shared our disappointment that John would not be part of the second study group. John even offered to pay the costs involved in the program to be included. This showed his poignant desperation. The oncologist sympathized with him, but paying out of pocket was not an option. Time was critical. Treatment needed to start—immediately. I felt as if we were racing against a fateful clock, competing in a risky race with cancer the only dangerous competitor. In the back of my mind, I knew the outcome of this deadly competition, and John was not going to be declared the winner.

We were told that treatment would have to begin immediately after his diagnosis, or he'd only have four weeks of life. We were in week three. I cannot speak for John, nor did we have this discussion, but deep down, I believe John thought he might be one of the lucky few who could live another year or two with or without being part of a study. Despite the tragic diagnosis and rejection from two trial opportunities, John's positivity and hopefulness continued.

The minutes were rapidly ticking away, and we were truly running out of time to begin treatment. The tumors were growing faster than the minute hand on an analog clock. It was determined that John would receive six weeks of chemotherapy and six weeks of radiation simultaneously, the standard treatment for anyone with GBMs. Things were unfolding and progressing so fast; it was all I could do to keep up with our calendar, doctor appointments, medical forms, health insurance paperwork, John's sales business, our personal venture, phone calls, emails, mail, and routine chores and responsibilities. I never had time to thoroughly process our heartbreaking circumstances; I bounced from one issue to the next to complete whatever needed to be done just to get through the day. It was as if John and I were playing Chutes and Ladders, and our tokens repeatedly landed on the chutes, always missing the ladders.

The head radiologist was amazing in swiftly pushing John through the sluggish system so that radiation could begin. I was very grateful since a trial was not in the cards. We were entering yet another unanticipated uproar of uncertainty, and I prayed we could ride it out. Our lives seemed to be taking on more water than we could bail out of our jerry-rigged, leaky boat. John and I sent out another mass email to update family, friends, and business associates on the game plan (chemotherapy and radiation) and stated our need for privacy during this troubling time; we could not wrap our heads (a poor choice of words) around our devastating situation.

First on the to-do list was to get a mask made of John's face so radiation treatment could start. I had no idea how this mask would be made, the exact purpose, or specifically, the intended use of it; this was yet another educational lesson I wish I did not have to discern. An appointment was scheduled a few days later for the mask to be made. When we arrived in the radiation department, John was brought to a private room to begin the process. When he returned to the waiting room, John explained that a lightweight, string-like mesh and pliable putty solution was applied to his face, quickly hardening into an individualized mold that was removed and cleaned and accurately fit his face. The result was a personalized, three-dimensional net face covering labeled with John's name and date of birth that would be kept in the radiation department and used when he received treatment. Surprisingly, the process was quite simple and painless. John was ready to start radiation treatment and chemotherapy at home at the same time. I felt some relief and comfort that an actual plan was in place.

Radiation treatments would be Monday through Friday for six weeks, and we were asked what time worked best in our schedule for the daily regimen. We chose 3:20 p.m. so our mornings would be quiet and low-key. John could take it easy after lunch, and we would hopefully be out of the downtown area by 5 p.m. to avoid rush hour traffic. Despite this grievous time, we could not have asked for more caring and compassionate health-care workers, from the oncologist, staff, head radiologist, and receptionist to the valet parking attendants. Their warmth and kindness helped make our unfortunate turn of events somewhat tolerable.

The hospital valet service was a true blessing. An attendant greeted us each time we pulled up to the side entrance of the hospital, helping John out of our car and into a hospital wheelchair. We got to know one worker well, and he always greeted John with, "Good afternoon, Mr. Hart. It's good to see you today." He knew which hospital wheelchair I preferred (in my opinion, the pink ones were the easiest to maneuver, yet I'm sure they were all the same). When he saw us pull up a little after 3 p.m., he would grab a pink wheelchair for John. Once John was settled in the chair, we made our way through the hospital corridors, to the elevators, and down to the radiation department on a lower floor, where John checked in with the receptionist before we entered the waiting room. I made sure John took on the check-in responsibility to keep his mind alert and engaged.

We saw the same patients and families almost every afternoon. Everyone was assigned a specific treatment time, patients ranging from about eighteen to eighty-five. Some people were approachable and cordial, and we casually talked about the weather or plans for the upcoming weekend. Others were private and would occasionally nod their heads when we made eye contact. Those who engaged in conversation rarely discussed the type of cancer their loved one or friend was being treated for, which I found somewhat unusual. Perhaps I was more open to these exchanges than most people. I found many patients and their families to be absorbed by their own concerns and worries. During our time in the waiting room, I was surprised by the number of jail inmates passing by, accompanied by guards, and escorted to a designated area to await radiation treatment. I discovered there was a separate hospital entrance for inmates for tests or treatments. This observation never would have occurred to me before.

At 3:20 p.m. on Mondays through Fridays, a technician entered the waiting area and pushed John to the radiation treatment room. I was very curious about the process. After the first treatment, John explained that two hospital aides lifted him out of the wheelchair and positioned him on his back on the examination table. A bolster was placed under John's knees, and his feet, arms, and chest were strapped down. John's personalized mask was placed over his face and snapped to the table. It fit snug and tight; there was no give to move his head. The mask had to be confining as radiation was only directed to the specific tumor. If John's head was not accurately positioned, radiation could damage surrounding areas of the brain. Once he was situated on the table and his head properly aligned, the technician stepped into a nearby control center. Computer software allowed an exact fix on the tumor where radiation would be directed. If the graphics did not precisely line up, the treatment table would be adjusted from a computer program. Once the alignment was one-hundred-percent accurate, John was told over an intercom that treatment would begin. The technician observed John from a monitor, and he was told to raise his hand if there were any issues. Loud rock music played over a speaker to give the patient something to focus on. John mentioned a new hit song that played during his first treatment. I still feel a sense of sadness whenever I hear this song.

The whole process took about twenty to twenty-five minutes. The actual radiation was about ten to fifteen minutes. I could only imagine the claustrophobia and discomfort of the mask, but John said he got used to it and found the time somewhat relaxing.

Following the treatment, we returned to the valet and waited for our car. Again, the attendants were very kind, which made our trying time somewhat bearable. The workers were cheerful and happy to help John into the car. On hot days, the attendant made sure the air-conditioning was on full force to keep us comfortable on our drive home.

On the third day of treatment, John asked the technician if I could accompany him to the radiation area to get a firsthand look. I was shocked and stunned when I entered the room. The first thing that came to mind was Frankenstein's ghoulish workshop. I found the number of face masks and body casts startling. Very eerie. Once John was settled on the treatment table, in the proper position, the technician let me stand outside the control room to watch the computer align graphics with the large tumor to begin radiation. I was asked to return to the waiting room while the technician started and monitored the treatment.

There is evidence that the combination of radiation and chemotherapy is most effective in treating GBMs or preventing further tumor growth. A trial may add further hope when treating this sneaky, deadly cancer; sadly, John was not accepted into the two trials to which we applied. Without question, I was terrified when John had to begin chemotherapy at home on the same day as his first radiation treatment. Chemotherapy was in pill form. The pills were overnighted and delivered to our front door, and someone had to be home to sign for the parcel. It was unsettling to see the skull and crossbones symbols and *TOXIC* on the packaging.

The oncologist's office strongly impressed upon me that *timing* was the fundamental key to anyone receiving chemotherapy in pill form. I am a bona fide rule follower, so rigid timing was not difficult for me. After dinner every night, no matter what time we ate, we waited a certain amount of time before I gave John the *special* pill, which warded off bad side effects associated with chemotherapy. A certain amount of time after he took the special pill, I gave him the chemo pill. John often joked that I could be slowly poisoning him, as he was oblivious to the medications and drugs he was taking. I was the only one dispensing his vitamins, prescriptions, special pills, and chemo pills. We have had many laughs over the years as he took whatever tablets I set out for him, never questioning what they were. This perfectly describes our relationship, fun and lighthearted, no matter what challenges we were dealing with.

By this time, John was sleeping downstairs on the living room sofa. It was too difficult and unsafe to get him up and down the stairs to our bedroom with his dead right arm and gimpy right leg. I was okay with him sleeping on the sofa, but I did not want our living room turned into a hospital room setting. I suggested that an extra bed be moved downstairs to his office, but John was not on board. He said he felt comfortable sleeping on the sofa.

The first night John took the special pill and chemo tablet, I was more than ready for him to be sick. I had his phone programmed to call my cell phone if he needed me during the night; he just needed to press the *call* button. I prepared the sofa with sheets, a blanket, and John's pillow and surrounded the sofa with towels and a bowl in case he felt ill during the night. I placed damp washcloths in the refrigerator for John's forehead if he felt nauseous (an old-school remedy my mother instilled in me that I still swear by) and several in the freezer.

That evening, I got John comfortable on the sofa and went upstairs around 11 p.m. I woke up unexpectedly at 2:30 a.m., ran downstairs to check on him, and noticed he was sleeping like a baby. Whew. I went back to bed and fell right to sleep. The next morning, I was guardedly anxious to see how he was feeling. Thankfully, John had no side effects, but I kept up the routine for several weeks in case he had a bad spell as time went on. I quickly realized, as the oncologist said, that the schedule of the special pill and the chemo tablet was clearly all in the timing. Surprisingly, John never got sick from chemotherapy. We never altered the timing of the two pills, and that helped him feel as well as he did. I have a different outlook on chemotherapy after witnessing John with no bad side effects, but I realize everyone reacts differently to treatment.

John was pretty much homebound except for the Monday through Friday radiation treatments or medical appointments. Many afternoons, John wanted to go out for an early dinner following his radiation treatment. As each day passed, going out for a quick bite to eat became increasingly difficult. John was totally dependent on Big Red and Steady Eddy, with me overseeing his safety. The urgency to go out to eat or any other jaunt—the need for normalcy during an abnormal time—is common for someone with a serious illness, not knowing if he would be able to get out tomorrow, the next week, or even the next month, but it was difficult as a caregiver. I experienced this with my dad, so I understood. I tried to take John out to wherever he wanted to go for his sake, but it was difficult and challenging to tackle trips, given John's physical condition and limitations. Attempting meal outings was not easy, let alone the challenges we faced entering and leaving a restaurant. When we went for a bite to eat, I found people more than happy to hold restaurant doors or offer other assistance. I was very grateful for the kindness of strangers.

I was fortunate to be able to occasionally leave the house for thirty to forty-five minutes at a time (to go to the grocery store, a quick appointment, a club meeting, etc.), leaving John at home alone. I made sure he had gone to the bathroom and was settled in a chair or on the sofa with his cell phone accessible, the TV remote, and plenty of reading material before I headed out. Because John was so unsteady on his feet, he promised to stay put until I returned.

I truly did not know how I was going to get through most days with everything on my plate, and silently questioning whether the treatments were truly effective only compounded the fear of unknowns. The outpouring of support from family, friends, and neighbors was extremely heartwarming. Knowing that others were thinking about us and keeping us in their prayers made the days more bearable, whether it was receiving a thinking-of-you note, a short email or text of concern, food, or gifts on our porch. Many days, our mailbox was filled with cards of well-wishes addressed to John. Often, he would shake his head in utter disbelief and was frequently brought to tears by the number of cards he received in a day. Several times, he said, "It's okay for a grown man to cry, isn't it?" John was truly touched by the outpouring of support.

John continued having difficulty walking, especially navigating stairs. After a few weeks, I knew sleeping on the sofa could not be as comfortable as a bed. I made an executive decision, and Kevin and I moved an extra bed into John's office, which gave him easy access to a hallway powder room. Oh, how I wish we had a first-floor primary bedroom. John was not happy that we set up a bed downstairs, but I knew this was best. After the first night of sleeping in a bed again, John sheepishly admitted it was much more comfortable than the sofa. I made sure he was all set before I went upstairs. John had Steady Eddy by his bedside, and his cell phone was programmed to call me if he needed anything during the night. Most nights, he slept well, and I slept like a baby from the sheer exhaustion of taxing days and knowing John could reach me if needed.

Every night, I gave John his marching orders that he could not get up until I came downstairs at 6:45 a.m. I set my alarm for 6:30 each day, took a quick shower, dressed, and was ready for whatever lay ahead. Every day was a constant worry, wondering what might unexpectedly pop up; handling numerous phone calls, emails, and mail intensified the daily demands and uncertainties I was feeling, which frequently resulted in tremendous anxiety and stress. Many times, I wondered how I was going to get through the day. Sadly, John was unable to conduct work on the phone or computer, and he was totally dependent on me.

With stairs too difficult, we started every morning with a relaxing sponge bath in the downstairs powder room. It was a small half bath, so the door was removed to accommodate Big Red and Steady Eddy. After a week or so, we had the morning routine down to a tee. A friend, whose wife had passed away, offered to lend us several medical equipment items, including a shower seat, which I immediately accepted; it was definitely needed. I was able to get John upstairs a few more times for a warm, relaxing shower, which he relished.

One afternoon, John asked me to take him to get his hair trimmed. I cringed at this idea. It was physically difficult and dangerous to get him out of the house, in and out of the car, into Big Red, with him holding Steady Eddy, wheel him into wherever we were going, and return home. I begged John to let me trim his hair and clean up his neck and beard to avoid yet another arduous outing. He finally backed down and gave me free rein. With scissors and an electric razor, I went into stylist mode. I patted myself on the back for doing a fabulous job, and most importantly, John was really pleased with the results. Of course, I insisted on a big tip from such a happy customer! We were on a roll with his bathroom and salon undertakings. As challenging as this time was, I was adamant about keeping our everyday routines running as smoothly and low-key as possible, and I breathed a sigh of relief when I could accomplish daily troublesome tasks.

Late one afternoon, John and I were sitting at a table in a restaurant, enjoying a glass of wine after placing our dinner order with the server. While we were waiting for our meal to arrive, a couple we barely knew stopped by our table to speak to us. They were aware of John's diagnosis and asked how they could help. I replied, "Thank you. We are doing okay," and we had a short, pleasant conversation. Our dinner arrived, and the couple returned to their table. John and I enjoyed our meal and waited for the server to bring the bill. When the check did not come, I questioned the waitress, and she told us that another guest paid our bill. We were surprised and warmhearted that a couple we hardly knew paid for our dinner. We thanked them for their kindness and headed home. I will always remember their thoughtfulness.

Within a few weeks, it became impossible for us to safely venture out to eat. John was enfeebled. I could no longer help him in a restaurant setting, and it wasn't safe. It was all I could do to get John out of the house, in the car, in Big Red, and back into the house for radiation treatments, doctor visits, or crucial appointments. Even with Steady Eddy, John was very unstable and totally dependent on Big Red, and me for ordinary, everyday activities.

August 2015

Daniel graduated from college and returned home. John stayed behind while I picked Daniel up at the airport. It was important to John that Daniel see him standing in the living room as we entered the house. Although John was able to stand, he was off-balanced and noticeably weak. John had gone downhill tremendously since Daniel was home in early June, only two months earlier. John was using Steady Eddy on a regular basis, had an arm sling, a leg brace, and a gait belt, and required Big Red to get to the living room, powder room, his bed, and the car. John could no longer do the choo choo train shuffle.

Our days were long, extremely challenging, and overwhelming. I was barely getting through some days, pulling whatever little strength I had left, relying on my faith and commitment as a wife, best friend, and now full-time caregiver. Although I think of myself as a strong, resilient person, this period was a total nightmare for which I was unprepared to deal with and blindly navigating. This unsettling period was never on our life path.

The oncologist impressed upon me that anyone receiving radiation and chemotherapy simultaneously may be prone to internal bleeding should a fall occur. I did not obsess over this, but his comment was written down on a Post-it Note in the back of my mind. One night, I got John settled into bed around 9 p.m. All was quiet until I was suddenly awoken around 2 a.m. by a loud thud. I ran downstairs and found John on the floor next to his bed—a pool of blood surrounding his head. He was awake but unable to move. John was so weak from radiation that he had no strength to even try to get up, nor did he fully realize he had fallen and was bleeding.

When I first saw the large bloody puddle, the Post-it Note surfaced, and I reasoned he was bleeding internally. Possibly from his ear? After cleaning his face and assessing the injury, it was evident he had a 1.5-inch deep cut on his right eyebrow. The blood loss stopped when I applied pressure, so I knew John was not bleeding internally. He explained that he got up to go to the bathroom and fell, hitting his head on a side table. In John's condition, I did not feel the urgent need to take him to the ER for stitches. I bandaged his eyebrow, Daniel and I cleaned everything up, and we got John settled into bed before going back to sleep.

John was an independent sales representative, in the business for about forty-seven years. In late April 2015, he decided to slow down a bit and was training Kevin to take over several accounts. Kevin was excited about his new career opportunity and wanted to learn as much as he could from John. In early June, when John was diagnosed and was unable to handle daily phone calls, emails, etc., Kevin stepped up and blindly dove into the job. Hoping that John's health would be a temporary setback, we felt that John would be back on track once he felt up to it. Kevin did a wonderful job making sure all work-related matters were taken care of until John could return.

John and I had a thirty-five-plus-year joint venture that we developed and owned. John managed the day-to-day operations, and I oversaw paperwork, bookkeeping, and any other issues that arose. The business fell totally on me after John's diagnosis. This was an all-consuming responsibility that I attempted to operate myself. It was not too long before I recognized I could not run our business and care for John at the same time, so I turned the day-to-day operations over to a management company. This lifted some weight off my shoulders, but I was still accountable for handling certain aspects of the business and unexpected issues that cropped up. I was overwhelmed—fielding an abundant number of daily phone calls, emails, faxes, and mail for John's sales business, our personal company, and keeping up with routine obligations and demands at home. With challenges coming at me from every direction, I could not let John's sales business, our company, or home responsibilities collapse.

Each day presented a variety of unexpected undertakings. Many days, I could barely hold it together. Our lives had turned into a recalled defective pressure cooker, ready to burst at any moment. I knew I had to give myself an open-ended pass in every aspect of my life. Emotionally and physically, anxiety and unpredictability consumed me, and I felt smothered by helplessness and stress. I took a leave of absence from my part-time job and dropped out of all clubs, groups, committees, and classes.

Not knowing what the future held for his dad and our family, Daniel decided to live at home, help when needed, and search for a job in his field after graduation. Alyssa and Kevin were busy taking care of their newborn, who was a little over a month old. I had initially planned to help Alyssa and Kevin when Wyatt arrived, but there was no time to offer assistance to the new parents. They lived forty minutes away yet visited almost every day and assisted us. Daniel, Alyssa, and Kevin provided immediate help, and their support was immeasurable. Much later, I realized John and I were never able to fully savor our new roles as first-time grandparents.

Side effects from radiation, primarily extreme exhaustion, usually occur several weeks into the six-week treatment regimen. I was told that the fatigue can be so intense that a patient cannot even power through the lack of energy. Ready for what may come, we were surprised that the debilitating exhaustion hit John about ten days *after* the radiation treatments ended. I would get John to bed around 9 p.m., his set bedtime, and he would not wake up until 2 p.m. or later the next day. Many days, I struggled to wake him up late in the afternoon. Sleeping seventeen to eighteen straight hours was concerning. This went on for about ten days. I felt very unsettled and could not ignore his extreme lethargy and intense immobility.

Occasionally, I overheard John on the phone talking with

business associates or friends. Sometimes, his conversations did not make sense. Ultimately, I had to gingerly take his cell phone away to preserve his business and personal standing. Even talking to us, his immediate family, John's thinking was cloudy and muddled. One afternoon, a silent hunch continued to tug at me, indicating something was not right. I could not shake off these restless feelings. John's oncologist was out of town when I called to voice my worries, and I had to advocate hard to get him checked out at the hospital. When I was given the green light to bring John to the ER for an evaluation, I could not get him out of the house, even with Daniel's help. With John sitting in Big Red, Daniel and a friend of ours carried him to the car. Our battered boat was taking on massive amounts of water, and I continued to feel helpless and fearful as we were sinking further into deep despair. Was this another unexpected squall we could get through, let alone weather? Honestly, I knew I would survive this stormy time, but deep down, I knew John would not.

September 2015

Once John was admitted to the ER and my concerns were heard, an MRI of his brain was ordered. The MRI revealed that he continued to have massive swelling in the brain, a common side effect of radiation. John was already on a large dose of steroids to reduce the swelling, and he was given the highest safe amount. If I had not brought him into the ER when I did, the swelling likely would have continued to increase, pushing against the areas of the brain that control his breathing, organs, senses, and parts of the body. I am so thankful that I listened to my gut feeling.

I realized I was no longer equipped or physically able to care for John at home. I could no longer safely maneuver him from a bed or chair to Big Red, let alone manage to get him in and out of the house on my own. My back and body ached from steadying and lifting him throughout the day.

John spent his sixty-second birthday in the hospital while several professionals attempted to determine how best to treat him. There was no cake or gifts to honor his special day. I promised we would celebrate his birthday when he returned home. Well, that never happened. John spent the next few days in the hospital as the doctors worked to reduce the swelling and balance his unstable vitals. I had an outside commitment one afternoon, and I was grateful a friend offered to sit with John in his hospital room so I could get away for a few hours. Having my friend stay with John gave me much peace of mind; I did not want John to wake up from a nap wondering where he was, where I was, or when I might return.

Over the next several days, I agonized about what the next disconcerting development might be in this heartbreaking nightmare. Discussing options for John's care with numerous doctors, a social worker, the insurance company, and other health professionals was perplexing and indescribable. I could not bring John back home in his current condition as I was no longer able or equipped to care for him. I felt paralyzed and vulnerable. It was recommended that John be admitted to a rehabilitation facility to regain his strength and mobility from radiation. I could not believe the fast decline in John's physical state.

Several area inpatient rehab facilities were suggested to contend with his impairments. The hospital also had two inpatient rehab units, one for those suffering head injuries or brain issues and another for general rehab for those following a fall, stroke, accident, etc. I do not know why, but I was not gung ho on an outside facility. I asked to tour the hospital rehab unit for head/brain issues. My heart ached when I viewed the patients on-site for the essential care they required. This was a startling observation. I thought, *Is this what John's life has come to*? Oh, how I did not want to go in that direction.

I had to wait several days to hear if insurance would cover the cost of either unit and if there was a bed available. It was a troubling, agonizing wait, filled with considerable stress and topped with enormous uncertainty. Within a few days, insurance came through, and bed space was available in the general rehab unit. I thanked God for our directed path as we attempted to move forward—not knowing what moving forward really meant.

John was admitted Friday afternoon. I was thankful and relieved—and stunned at how quickly a body can regress without regular movement. Our lives seemed to be anchored in a bottomless, dark sea of questionable hope, with John getting the professional care he desperately needed.

The rehab unit was wonderful, well, as wonderful as it could be, given John's impediments. His assigned room was directly across from the large whiteboard with patients' last names, room numbers, daily schedules, etc. A warning sign was posted on John's door, citing he recently received chemotherapy, meaning his bodily fluids were toxic to others. This notice puzzled me. I never realized just how unsafe he was to others while receiving chemotherapy.

John was scheduled for occupational therapy one hour a day, physical therapy one hour a day, and speech therapy one hour a day. I was encouraged and hopeful when I learned that he would be receiving these sessions Monday through Friday. The initial plan was for John to be in the general rehab unit for a month; however, he was not happy when he learned this. I constantly reminded John to work hard at his therapy sessions, and the doctors would discharge him the minute they thought he was ready and able to return home.

We quickly learned that weekends were very relaxed. There were no therapy sessions, so Saturdays and Sundays were laid back and quiet. On that first Sunday, the physician on duty noticed we were new and explained that John could leave for an hour at a time—stroll the hallways, grab a bite to eat in the cafeteria, or go outside for fresh air—but we had to remain on the hospital grounds. I signed John out at the unit's reception desk. I was ready for a change of scenery, so we decided to head outside to enjoy the warm sunshine of the beautiful September day. As I pushed John through the double doors to an outdoor gathering space, a thought came to mind—*Will we be able to get back through those?*—but I brushed it aside. We sat outside the hospital, talking, people-watching, and enjoying the delightful fall day. A short time later, I glanced at my watch and realized we had been gone for almost an hour. I knew I needed to get John back to the rehab unit. Well, my initial thought was spot on. We could not get back in. *Ahh!* On weekends, the side doors were one-way. We could not help but laugh at our plight.

The main entrance was two blocks up a steep incline. The sidewalk was rough and uneven, making the trek arduous. I had to stop to catch my breath several times, putting the wheelchair brake on so John would not roll backward. We were late returning to the rehab unit, and I feared someone would come looking for us. I discovered there was no designated guard in this unit, so we could be lax with coming and going. John and I always had fun together, even when encountering unexpected bumps in the road. Those many laughs hold a special place in my heart.

Since John was admitted to the rehab unit late on a Friday afternoon, he had to wait until Monday to begin his sessions. The occupational therapist was a breath of fresh air, cheerful, kind, positive, and encouraging. She showed him how to bathe, dress, and feed himself, the everyday activities we all take for granted. John often struggled to accomplish tasks that used to be effortless, yet he worked hard at all the sessions.

The physical therapists vigorously pushed John during each appointment. He worked on how to get in and out of a bed, a wheelchair, a car, and up off the floor should a fall occur, as well as other normal activities. Some sessions required John to work out on a stationary bike, pedaling on a virtual mountain road up and down hills and ridges. Not only did this form of therapy sustain John's coordination and strengthen his leg muscles, but it also kept his mind engaged and alert. During other sessions, John was hooked up to a harness that assisted him in standing and walking. It was a major accomplishment when he walked eight to ten feet with the apparatus. The heartache of seeing John struggle with his physical therapy sessions was more than Daniel, Alyssa, Kevin, and I could emotionally withstand. We were there to root John on, and it broke our hearts when his attempts were sometimes unsuccessful.

I was enthusiastic and on board with John's occupational and physical therapy sessions, being his biggest cheerleader, but I was puzzled as to why speech therapy was included. John spoke well, with no slurred speech or blatant forgetful thoughts or memories. Yes, his thinking was noticeably foggy, but he had brain cancer and intense treatments that could have caused that. It wasn't until the third day of speech therapy that I realized how troubling things were. John seemed to be reading on a first-grade level, could not point to pictures of ordinary household items, and did not comprehend a calendar or why he needed to know the days of the week or year. It was hard to hear John struggle to sound out simple words or describe pictures of familiar objects. The speech therapist suspected the large tumor was touching the language area of the brain. I was totally shocked. *Were there early warning signs that I missed?*

Not only had John been a voracious reader from a young age, but he was also a numbers person, so it was heartbreaking to watch him struggle with basic knowledge. John was the one person you wanted as your phone-a-friend on *Who Wants to Be a Millionaire?* game show. He often joked that although he may be versed in many areas, much of what he knew was frivolous, auxiliary information. I thought back to mid-July and understood why John sat in the living room, not interested in doing anything. I believe the words in a book or newspaper were confusing, and he was unable to express this to me.

For the thirty days John was scheduled to be in the rehab unit, I arrived at the hospital around 9 a.m. and returned home between 7 and 8 p.m. Heartache and helplessness flooded my mind as I sat by John's bedside and accompanied him to his therapy sessions and the dining room for lunch and dinner. It was a depressing and dismal atmosphere. Deep down, I knew this was exactly where he needed to be, but it was an unpleasant period.

When I returned home at the end of the day, I was wiped out. I grabbed a quick bite from the refrigerator or freezer and dove into several hours of office work. I just couldn't seem to get a break in handling the day-to-day demands. Evil storm clouds hovered above me, with no clear skies in sight. As much as I hated every second of every minute of every hour of every day for the thirty consecutive days John was in the rehab unit, I would not have been anywhere else. John needed me, and I wanted to be there for him. We made the best of it, with several light moments and laughs, but we had many tough, challenging occasions, which will remain private.

One morning, when I arrived at the hospital, it was pouring down rain, and I felt like a research mouse in an experimental maze, winding my way through the hallways to the nearest elevators and dodging outside walkways to avoid getting drenched. The murky, dreary, stormy day put an additional emotional cloud over me. I had almost reached the rehab unit when I abruptly stopped in the middle of a hallway and broke down in tears. I could not stop crying. I was embarrassed to think someone might see me bawling. From day one of John's diagnosis, I managed to remain positive and kept my chin up, but the dam holding back my bottled-up emotions broke. Perhaps the gloomy, depressing, showery morning opened the floodgates. I will never forget standing in the hallway, trying to pull myself together before continuing to John's room, trusting no one saw me. Well, someone did see me uncontrollably sobbing. The woman stopped and asked what she could do. I shook my head, said, "Nothing," and thanked her; she went on her way. I was able to get myself together, wipe away the tears, pull my chin back up, and proceed to John's room.

Mondays through Fridays, the rehab unit was a flurry of activity. Ninety-nine percent of the patients had suffered a fall, a stroke, a heart attack, or an accident. During John's stay, he had two roommates.

The first roommate was an older gentleman who had cancer. He was discharged a few days later. I did not know his prognosis or where he went when he was released. John's second roommate was another elderly man with—if I recall correctly—stomach cancer. He rarely had visitors, so I always checked to see if there was anything I could do for him. He was a private person, who kept to himself. I wondered why he was there. I never saw him leave the room and suspected he was unable to care for himself at home.

One afternoon, as I was sitting by John's bedside, working on a cross-stitch project while he rested, two doctors entered the room and asked me to step out while they spoke privately to the roommate. I left the room and waited in a nearby lounge. When I returned to John's room, the doctors had left, and the room was quiet. I learned that the doctors advised the gentleman that there was nothing more they could do to help him survive the cancer. I do not think he had a lot of family or friends in the area, and I was sad to think he received this devasting news alone. When I arrived at the hospital a few days later, the gentleman was gone; he had been discharged.

One evening, after being at the hospital all day with John, Daniel and I went to Alyssa and Kevin's house for dinner. On the drive, Daniel questioned how long the doctors thought his dad had brain cancer. I told him the doctors suspected six to nine months prior to the first sign—the clumsiness of John's right arm. This was a huge lightbulb moment for me, which I had never fully put together, the tragic diagnosis clouding my mind. It was simple math, and if the tumors had been growing for six to nine months and the life expectancy for someone with GBMs is twelve to fifteen, *Were we looking at John living maybe another three months?*

Many days, I felt like John and I were unpaid extras on a TV hospital drama. The rehab unit was a nonstop bustle of activity, and we witnessed several unexpected, unusual incidences. Patients were constantly going to and from therapy sessions or other personalized programs. We met nurses throughout the day, who we enjoyed talking with, anything to take our minds off our bleak situation. It was interesting to hear how they ended up working in the rehab unit as opposed to other areas of the hospital. One nurse told us that over the course of twenty years in the field, she had worked in a variety of departments in the hospital. She found the rehab unit especially rewarding, seeing some patients greatly improve and return home. Hearing this, my heart sank. I knew this was not going to be the case with John. There was not going to be a happy ending. During his stint in rehab, I marveled at John's positive attitude and willingness to work hard in his therapy sessions. It did not surprise me. That was John's personality, a cheerful and upbeat mindset. I admired his zeal with his life flashing right before us, yet I am not sure John was fully aware that his life was nosediving.

There were many instances when John was alert and coherent, and no one would guess he had brain cancer. However, there were also many times his mind was in a complete fog. John recognized his doctors, nurses, aides, and therapists, yet he repeatedly whispered to me, "Now, what's their name?" Several minutes later, he would ask me the same question. It was important to John to call someone by their name, but he could not recall it even after I had reminded him. I frequently told John not to worry about it; a friendly hello was perfectly fine.

One afternoon, John and I were talking about our home, and he remarked that he could not remember what our home looked like, which was disturbing. Again, this showed me how cloudy his thinking was. I reminded him that we had lived in our home for twenty-six years, that it was a brick house, and that it sat up on a hill with a blacktop driveway. He seemed puzzled, so I offered to take a picture of our home and show it to him the following day, hoping to spark recollection. When I returned, I showed him the picture, and he said, "Oh, now I remember."

Many days, I arrived to find John upset that his coffee had gotten cold and *they* (the nurses/aides/staff) had not come to his room to heat it up. He said he had buzzed them many times, but no one appeared. I explained numerous times that he was in the hospital and that it was not the staff's responsibility to warm up anyone's coffee. I do not think John understood. I believe he thought he was in a restaurant, obviously not happy with the service. Understandably, the staff had more important things to do. I did whatever I could to smooth things over with the workers; I did not want John flagged as a difficult patient.

For the last six to eight weeks, I kept my cell phone and John's with me to maintain business and personal communications. They rang constantly, which added stress every day to keep up with the calls or messages. I felt like a crazed switchboard operator from the early 1900s, bouncing from one call to the next. Soon after John was admitted to rehab, I forwarded all his sales calls and emails to Kevin, which gave me a little break, but it took time, which I did not have, to write down the phone numbers and messages and relay the information to him. Although we were enduring tragedy, I could not let John's sales business or our personal company fall apart; I had to keep up with all communications in a timely manner.

Early on, when overseeing John's cell phone calls, I was extremely irritated when I discovered he had less than ten telephone numbers programmed in his phone. He was a numbers person and knew 95 percent of business associates', colleagues', and friends' phone numbers by heart. In the past, when a call came to John's cell phone, he would see the number and immediately know who was calling. I always marveled at that gift, but it made it difficult for Kevin and me. I had no idea who was calling, especially when the caller did not leave a name or speak clearly. I was often totally in the dark.

John was not cognizant enough to carry on a business conversation or respond to communications, and I kept his cell phone and laptop away from him for these reasons. Several weeks into John's rehab stay, I was pushing him to the dining room for lunch when he demanded to check his cell phone. He was convinced

I was not keeping up with phone calls and emails. We had a heated argument in the hallway; I thought someone would call security. I finally gave John his phone. After he checked it for outstanding calls and other correspondence, he realized there were no messages or emails. Kevin and I were on top of everything. John apologized. I totally understood how he must have felt, wondering if calls and emails were piling up unanswered.

Breakfast was delivered to the patient's room. Patients could choose their breakfast, lunch, and dinner from a menu and turn in their choices for the next day. John had a good appetite, for which I was thankful. Lunch and dinner were brought to the rehab dining room for most of the patients. I packed my lunch every morning before I left the house and ate with John.

The dining room was eye-opening. Meals were served at the patient's table. There was no assigned aide or nurse to make sure patients had what they needed. I often saw patients struggle to open a milk carton, unwrap a straw, cut their food, or spread butter on a roll. Some were missing a fork, spoon, napkin, etc. Every day, I made the rounds, making sure everyone was assisted or had what they needed to eat their meal. It was hard to watch patients attempt day-to-day tasks we all take for granted, yet I knew they needed to undertake mealtime challenges.

A few weeks into John's stay, the physical therapist told me I needed to have a wheelchair ramp at the house when John returned home; I am sure the therapist questioned the stunned look on my face. Since John was wheelchair-dependent, a ramp was imperative to get him safely in and out of the house. This suggestion just about sent me over the edge. I was so overwhelmed with my already full plate that I could not fathom adding one more thing. I had no idea where to even look for, let alone purchase, a wheelchair ramp. After mentioning this dilemma to a friend, she told me not to worry; she and her husband would investigate ramps and get back to me. Several days later, I returned home to find that my friends had built a ramp on our back deck. In fact, they told me they did not like the incline of the first ramp, so they rebuilt it. With tears of appreciation and gratitude, I could not thank my friends enough. I realized there are true angels among us. A hospital valet attendant made a point to visit John when he was in the rehab unit, which was special and uplifting. I will always remember his kindness.

A woman passing us in the hallway one afternoon approached me and asked to speak to me privately. I parked John in his wheelchair near a nurses' station and stepped aside. She said, "I overheard your conversation with your husband the other day, and I just want to say that I'm sure this time must be difficult for you." Her comment caught me off guard. I had no idea what she was referring to. I did not even think to ask her what she heard. I tried to think back and could not recall anything that would have elicited that remark. I did not know who she was—a hospital worker or family member of a rehab patient? *What did she hear me say?* I was embarrassed to think she could have heard an argument between us, or was it something else? After that, I was mindful of what I said outside of John's hospital room.

John made decent strides in occupational, physical, and speech therapy—learning how to get in and out of bed, a wheelchair, a car, and up off the floor—until the third week of September. He backpedaled, seemingly forgetting everything he had learned. The therapists and I exchanged looks of alarm and doubt. I was distressed. John was going downhill—fast. After a lengthy consultation with the oncologist, expressing the therapist's and my concerns, an MRI revealed the tumors growing and swelling in his brain. This was devastating news, a report I did not expect to hear. I felt certain the six weeks of chemotherapy and radiation treatments would have shrunk the tumors to some extent or kept them at bay. Instead, the approach seemed worthless. Well, the treatments were not totally ineffective since they possibly extended John's life for a few months, but after six weeks of chemo and radiation, I thought the tumors would have shrunk a little. Bottom line? The cancer was taking over his brain, and there was nothing more that could be done to turn this horrific nightmare around. The rough, high tides had turned in an unfavorable direction.

I met with John's oncologist, the head of the radiation department, and other medical experts to get their thoughts and opinions on the appropriate route to take. Each one said there was nothing more that could be done to shrink the tumors and save John's life. The ticking clock had stopped, and we ran out of options. The head radiologist was wonderful, allowing John to remain in the rehab unit for a couple more days, taking up bed space, while my family decided the appropriate plan of action. Furious winds had dramatically changed, pushing us into yet another unanticipated direction of foreboding darkness.

Even though John's diagnosis was a death sentence from day one, I could not believe we needed to consider end-of life arrangements. Another trial option was presented, which sounded unusual and somewhat barbaric. I felt hesitant to go in that direction. When I asked the oncologist what he would do if John was his brother, he adamantly recommended we bring him home in a hospice program. Making this kind of final determination for a loved one—my husband and best friend—was agonizing and heartbreaking.

After much thought and thorough consideration, my children and I took the advice of the oncologist. John was not going to beat this devious, fatal cancer. I was told that most terminally ill patients enter hospice late. There is evidence to support that the sooner someone enters hospice, the longer they live. The degree of care is better and more palpable in a home setting. I met with a hospice representative to learn more about the program and begin the grievous process. The representative might have well been talking to a brick wall; I could not absorb what she was saying about the program and how it worked. I could not believe I was discussing my husband's end-of-life plan with a total stranger. To bring John home, a new wheelchair was ordered and delivered to the hospital so we would be all set when the release papers were signed. Gale force winds fiercely howled, tossing our rickety, sinking boat out of control, and shaking all my brittle emotions. Not only did our perilous boat seem to be weighed down by hopelessness and gut-wrenching despair, but my spirit and faith had also submerged.

The day-to-day struggles I continued to endure were demanding and taxing, emotionally and physically. Our terrible nightmare kept recurring. It was as if our small two-person boat mysteriously vanished in the middle of the ocean for four months and was rocked in a deep, dark, cold sea of mournful quandary; John and I were lost in total darkness. I felt alone, helpless, hopeless, powerless, vulnerable, and fearful, a frightful combination of complicated emotions I have never experienced. This was the darkest time in my life. I do not believe anyone is ever prepared to care for a terminally ill person, and I certainly was not. I truly could not wrap my head (again, another terrible choice of words) around our fateful circumstances.

October 2015

On the first Friday in October, it was a dreary, drizzly evening when the discharge papers were signed, releasing John from the rehab unit. As we prepared to leave the hospital, I was told John may only live about two or three more weeks. When the valet attendant brought our car to the side entrance of the hospital, John did not have the strength to stand or try to get into the car. Two hospital aides had to physically lift him out of the wheelchair and into the car. John was in a complete fog that rainy night. He was already on the highest dose of steroids, which seemed to only help a little with reducing the swelling in his brain. John was incoherent on the drive home; there was no conversation between us. When I pulled into the driveway and parked the car, Daniel and Kevin had to transport John out of the car and into the wheelchair, pushing him up the new ramp and into the house. Little did we realize, it would be the only time John used the newly ordered wheelchair and ramp. We entered the house and waited for the hospice representative to arrive. My mind was so jumbled that night. I do not even remember what we had for dinner or if we ate at all.

Once John was home, I had no idea if I could do what was necessary to care for someone terminally ill, whatever that entailed. The wind was at our backs, thrusting us deeper into another ominous, emotional, and physically deadly storm, and I knew there was no chance of surviving. Friends told me they could not believe how strong I was. *What?* I did not feel strong at all. In fact, the emotional weight was so heavy that I could barely get through each day. I certainly do not think I did anything different or special. To me, you deal with what is on your plate. Enough said.

The hospice representative arrived at the house about 8:30 that Friday night, and I was grateful she came out on such a cold, dreary night. It was paramount that John be immediately enrolled in the program so care could be provided if an emergency occurred during the night or over the weekend. She described how hospice worked and asked what type of medical equipment John needed. I knew I wanted a hospital bed and a bedside table; I wasn't sure what else might be useful. The bed and table would be delivered and set up the next day. The representative explained that a hospice nurse would be assigned to us and would stop by once a week to check on John, take his vitals, and answer any questions I might have. An aide would come to the house twice a week to bathe John and change the bedsheets. A hospice social worker would be in touch. John was in the room when the spokesperson went over the information, but I know he didn't understand why this stranger was in our home.

A comfort kit was ordered and would be delivered to the house. This kit contained many drugs and medications and was to be refrigerated as soon as it arrived. I was to call the hospice helpline to let them know I received it. When the representative left, I got John into the bed in his office, and I slept on the sofa downstairs to be nearby. I went to sleep trying to wrap my head (yes, poor phrasing again) around what had transpired over the past few months. Four months ago, John and I were living a balanced, carefree life, and without any warning, tragedy struck. *John was in hospice? What the hell?*

The next morning, Daniel and I rearranged the living room furniture to accommodate the hospital bed and bedside table. I decided to have them in the living room so John would be around the family and have access to the television; so much for not wanting our living room transformed into a hospital setting. The bed and table were set up quickly and in working order.

I sent out a mass email to let family, friends, business associates, neighbors, and others know that John had returned home and was in a hospice program. Again, I asked for privacy, and for the most part, my request was honored. It was important to create a quiet, low-key environment for John's final days. Occasionally, I found cards, flowers, gifts, and food on our porch or by the side door. One friend sent me a gift certificate for a ready-to-eat meal service. I ordered meals two nights a week, which gave me a little break from cooking. A meal team was offered to me, but I felt uneasy accepting it. I am more comfortable giving than receiving. I had to learn to welcome help—I truly needed additional assistance—but it was hard for me.

The outpouring of support from loved ones, friends, neighbors, and business associates was heartwarming, many times unexpected, and truly gave me the strength to get through the day. It meant a lot to me to know others were thinking about us and keeping us in their prayers. I felt that John and I were cared for during the darkest time in our lives. We managed to get through that first weekend fairly well while I tackled keeping our daily routine as normal as possible.

The hospice nurse arrived early Monday morning. When I opened the front door, the invisible bubble over my head read, *Did your mommy just drop you off, and she'll come pick you up when you're done?* She appeared extremely young, but after talking with her for about an hour, I felt more comfortable. Of course, she had the requisite qualifications and training to be a hospice nurse. She went over the comfort kit and explained the specific drugs and how to administer them. I took a lot of detailed notes but felt extremely apprehensive and unsure about administering them. The nurse told me to call her any time I had questions; she said she would return the following Monday to check on John. Never in my life did I feel more alone and scared.

We took each day as it came and dealt with unexpected challenges that occurred. John rested and slept a lot, and we would converse when he felt up to it. He was in good spirits, yet he did not realize he was in a hospice program or that he would be living out his last days at home. With help, I could move him into a chair to give him a break from lying in the hospital bed all day. Alyssa and Kevin bought John an exercise bike apparatus to continue his physical therapy and keep up his strength. It was a simple piece of equipment that sat on the floor. John could use it while seated in a chair. At mealtime, John had a good appetite, and I fixed him whatever he wanted, nutritious or not.

From the beginning of John's diagnosis, I was adamant about keeping a regular routine so there was no question how each day played out. I was sleeping downstairs on the sofa, setting my alarm for 6:30 every morning, running upstairs, taking a quick shower, and dressing. Most mornings, John was awake at 6:45 a.m. I raised the upper part of the hospital bed, adjusted the lower section, fluffed his pillows, and started breakfast while he watched the morning news.

Bedsores are a major concern for those with limited mobility or who are bedridden. Throughout the day, I adjusted the upper and lower sections of the bed to different levels to make sure John was comfortable, constantly propping pillows under his arms, legs, feet, and behind his back, anything to keep the blood circulating and prevent bedsores.

If he was up to it, he worked out on the bike pedal machine, which was good mental and physical therapy. At 9:00 p.m., it was teeth brushing time, and I flattened John's bed and told him to get to sleep. I dimmed the lights in the living room and spent several hours keeping up with chores and listening and responding to phone messages, emails, and mail. Thankfully, John slept well most nights. Not surprisingly, I had no trouble sleeping from the busy, challenging days and mental and physical fatigue. This routine continued for sixty-three uninterrupted days.

Occasionally, when I walked past the front door, I noticed that someone had left something on our porch. We continued to receive support from friends, neighbors, and business associates, which made me feel a little less alone. One business associate of John's sent him six or seven cards of concern over four months. Seeing the warmth on John's face each time he opened a note from her showed me the impact a note can have on someone going through a troubling period.

On the mantel and bookcases lining our living room fireplace, I displayed the countless cards John received. He received so many that I ran out of space to display them, so I doubled and even tripled up the cards on the bookshelves and mantel. Seeing the number of cards John received was heartwarming. John remarked several times that he felt like he was at his own funeral, with the outpouring of love, support, and prayers extended to him. Little did he realize, this was a preview of his soon-to-be funeral service.

Late one morning, about a week after John entered the hospice program, out of the blue, he became extremely agitated and said, "Am I going to be in this bed for the rest of my life?"

I was stunned. It took me a few minutes to consider how to respond. I answered, "Well, do you remember last June that you were diagnosed with brain cancer?"

He thought about what I said for several minutes, looking around the room, and replied, "Yes."

I continued, "Well, do you remember a hospice representative came to the house last Friday?"

John took a few moments before he responded, "Yes."

I said quickly and matter-of-factly, "Well, everything is going to be fine. Now, what can I fix you for lunch?" John settled down and never said another word about it. This brief, heartbreaking exchange brought me to tears. How on earth do you answer that sort of question, especially to your spouse? I have heard health-care workers state that it is important to be truthful with anyone who is gravely ill, perhaps to bring their thinking into reality, yet I did not think this was the time for honesty. John's reasoning continued to be fuzzy, and to me that was a good thing, considering his incurable illness. The thought of John lying in a hospital bed, knowing he would die any time from brain cancer, was unfathomable. Maybe I should have been candid and explained that he would soon pass away, but it did not serve any consequential purpose, so I kept quiet.

John had many alert moments, but he also did not know what day it was or where he was; his mind was in a complete fog. He was comfortable being at home and around our family, but if someone asked him what my name was or where he was, I don't know if he could answer. I was okay with this. My concern was to keep John comfortable, content, and safe.

The second week, the nurse returned on Monday. Her visits were routinely thirty to forty-five minutes long, checking John's vitals and answering my questions. The aide arrived for the first time to give John a sponge bath and change the bedsheets. She was a sweet, compassionate woman, very kind, and loving. I could not imagine how she was going to change the sheets. It seemed like a magic trick, watching her maneuver John to change the linens and bathe him. I quickly picked up on all her caregiving tips. I was doing several loads of laundry every day and could give John a sponge bath and change the sheets myself when the aide was not scheduled. I looked forward to her stopping by as she was always cheerful and upbeat, and John enjoyed her visits and tenderness. As the aide was leaving one of her visits, John whispered, "I love you," which made us tear up. He truly delighted in the care and compassion she provided.

Our routines were running smoothly, and we were handling our bleak situation rather well. I never let myself fall apart. I did not have the time. I took our predicament in stride, knowing this was the biggest crisis I would ever endure, well, hopefully. This was a part of life, good or bad, and unfortunately, I was on the receiving end of bad.

The hospice social worker stopped by the second week in October, but I did not feel the services were needed. I was on my own, with the help of Daniel, Alyssa, and Kevin. I truly could not have gotten through it without their assistance. They were willing and ready to lend hands-on support, but I was adamant to I carry the heaviest weight of John's care.

The first couple of weeks in hospice, John had a pretty good appetite. However, as each day passed, it became increasingly difficult to get him to eat anything. His body was shutting down, a natural progression for someone nearing death. Often, he was just not hungry or thirsty, and we were faced with him possibly choking as the main tumor was affecting his ability to swallow. It was challenging to come up with soft foods that were also nutritious. Many days, I felt lucky to get John to eat just a few bites or drink any kind of liquid.

About three weeks after leaving rehab, John fell into a trance-like, deep sleep. There were some disturbing concerns, and I called the hospice helpline to voice my worries. I am not the type to cry wolf at the drop of a hat, yet I continued to feel unsettled and unnerved. I called the helpline again later that night, and a nurse was dispatched to our home. We were having a torrential rainstorm, and I felt bad that a nurse was awoken in the middle of the night in a downpour. *Hmmm . . . what is with the recent rain in my life?*

The nurse arrived about 12:45 a.m. After describing the signs I witnessed, he did a thorough check of John's vitals and reassured Daniel and me that everything appeared normal for someone in John's state. The nurse spent almost two hours explaining what to expect when a body begins to shut down. His visit was extremely helpful and put us at ease. I was grateful for his time and insights, and

Daniel and I were able to get a few hours of sleep before our routine started up again the next morning. Oh, how I desperately wanted to wake up from this horrific nightmare.

In mid-October, knowing John may not live much longer, I slipped away one afternoon to investigate two cemeteries and begin the distasteful arrangements at a nearby funeral home. I had been through this process for my parents, so I knew I needed to get a handle on end-of-life preparations while my head was somewhat clear.

At the first cemetery, the representative asked what I was looking for in a gravesite; I had not previously given any consideration to this question. I did not expect a warm and fuzzy connection with the cemetery spokesperson, but his appearance and mannerisms were relatable to a shady con man or back-alley drug dealer. He drove me to various sections on the grounds, we got out of his car, and we walked to available plots. All I could express was that I will know the spot when I *feel* it. I felt very uneasy and uncomfortable. After looking at several sites, I stated that I needed to give more thought to the locations I saw, and I quickly hightailed it out of there. Even though I knew the afternoon would be emotional, I felt very discouraged as I thought picking out a gravesite would have been simple.

I drove to another cemetery—one with a good, long-standing history—and met with their representative. The agent was more professional and forthcoming. I was asked what type of gravesite I had in mind. Again, I said I would know when I *felt it*. We drove to several locations on the cemetery grounds. After about forty-five minutes, one spot felt right, and I said, "This is it." This spot spoke to me, and the location felt right. The site was near a well-manicured green hedge in a secluded area, so I felt visitors would not be traipsing on the gravesite. I also thought the location would be easy for our family to locate many years down the road. The representative and I returned to his office to complete the paperwork. I purchased two plots, one for John and one for me. Once the cemetery decision was in place, it was time to stop by the funeral home.

I had been to one specific funeral home on several occasions, which made the decision easy. I felt somewhat comfortable there. *Humph . . . can you really feel comfortable at a funeral home?* The appointment was more emotional than I envisioned. The representative went over the procedures of funeral planning. When it was time to pick out a casket, I felt sick to my stomach. Walking through the sizeable, haunting room, there were so many choices. I felt confused and overwhelmed. After a short time, one casket looked appropriate, and I completed the paperwork to finalize the arrangements. I returned home feeling pleased and relieved that most of the preparations were set.

After the doctors speculated that John might only live two or three weeks, I felt we were barely treading water as we passed week three. It was an ominous, precarious feeling. I felt weighed down by deep despair, paralyzed, defenseless, sinking in emotional turmoil, barely able to come up to the surface for air. There was no escaping the pain and sorrow. Unless someone has experienced it, no one can imagine how agonizing and gut-wrenching it is to see their life partner decline in health, slowly slipping away as organs and senses shut down.

November 2015

John had been home for four weeks. Each day, our lives crumbled more than the day before. I will never get over the shock of John's brain cancer diagnosis. It came out of the blue, hard to grasp and process. My emotions shifted from vulnerability and despair to edgy and fearful. Heartache, indescribable sadness, and helplessness swallowed me up. I felt suffocated by grief, and John was still alive.

Family members and friends were surprised that the only outside help we received was a forty-five-minute visit once a week from the hospice nurse and a thirty-minute visit twice a week from the hospice aide to bathe John and change the bedsheets—only one and a half hours of help each week. I believe when people learn that someone is in hospice, it is assumed a health-care worker is with the patient and/or the family most of the day. This was not the case, at least with us. Our days were long, tiring, emotionally and physically challenging, stressful, and draining. I know others care for a loved one longer than us, sometimes for many years, and it is hard to comprehend the struggles they are up against. I am fortunate that our family and friends reached out and expressed they were thinking of us and praying for John and me. It meant the world to me that others were concerned about us and lifting us up in prayer. The support truly gave me the strength to get through each day.

On several occasions, I experienced unannounced visitors, which added more tension and anxiety. As much as I appreciated their concern, their visits were often at inopportune times. I felt bad turning some people away, knowing they were worried about us. However, my top priority was John, ensuring he was comfortable and content and providing him with a calm, safe, low-key environment. It was important that our days were quiet and ran smoothly.

Several times, comments were made to me from visitors or in John's presence, which were totally inappropriate and just plain angered me. I was dealing with my husband nearing death, and the remarks were insensitive and unwarranted. I will never forget these words, which only compounded further pain, sadness, and anguish. As much as I tried to keep our lives normal, our lives had not been normal for months. Each day was a struggle. John was slipping away as every hour of every day passed.

Thanksgiving arrived. The holiday was far from typical. I roasted a turkey and had all the fixings for the traditional feast. There was no festive table set. Instead, my family filled their plates with the usual Thanksgiving celebratory dishes. We sat near John's hospital bed with our full plates on trays. Despite my reminders, John was not cognizant of the holiday festivities.

For as long as I can remember, at the beginning of every celebratory meal, John always reminded us that we have a lot to be thankful for; it is easy to take family, friends, and life for granted, and there is always someone less fortunate. His remarks were missed that holiday. I thought, *What do I have to be thankful for?* It was heart-wrenching. I did not want to accept this as the last Thanksgiving our family would spend with John. We did what we needed to get through the holiday. Truthfully, I could hardly wait for the day to be over.

December 2015

On Thursday, December 3, the aide arrived to bathe John and change the sheets. A caring and compassionate person, this was her true calling. As she was getting ready to leave that day, she discreetly pulled me aside and whispered about signs she viewed that John was nearing death. I was completely caught off guard. Despite being told John may only live another two to three weeks, when he was discharged from the rehab unit in early October, we were in week nine. I did not notice anything different with John, so I dismissed her remark and said, "Have a good weekend. I'll see you next Tuesday." The aide put on her coat, said her goodbyes, and gave me a distinct, heartfelt look that I had not seen from her before.

Alyssa joined us for dinner and said she noticed something different too. After many up-and-down days, I took her observation with a grain of salt, brushing aside Alyssa's account.

The next morning, December 4, I woke up at 6:30. John was awake and quiet, yet he seemed out of it. I raised the upper section of his bed, fluffed up and rearranged the pillows, and turned on the TV to the morning news, which I had done once he returned home from the rehab unit in early October. He did not seem ready for breakfast, so I told him I was going into the kitchen to grab a bite to eat and would return to check on him. When I came back to the living room only ten minutes later, John was gone. I never heard a sound from him. I waited for a few minutes to make sure he had actually passed away before waking Daniel up. We stood by John's side for several minutes, looking for signs of life, but there were none. I called the hospice nurse, and she came to the house and pronounced John dead. He passed away so peacefully; we should all be that lucky.

John ended up living for nine weeks—sixty-three days. I believe home care contributed to him living longer than expected. John would have a good day or two, and I'd be hopeful things might improve, but a few days later, his condition would be so poor that I did not think he would make it through the night. Each day, I felt like I was riding on an archaic, rickety, wooden roller coaster, whipping my emotions at every turn with fear, anxiety, and trepidation, not to mention terribly challenging moments; this was a park ride I never wanted to be on.

I often hoped to wake up to find that John had passed away in his sleep. I did not know what his death would be like. Would he be anxious? Gasp for breath? Choke? Experience excruciating pain?

I was able to reach Kevin on his way to an appointment, and he came straight to the house. Kevin and Daniel drove to Alyssa's workplace to deliver the news and bring her to the house. It was important to me that Alyssa and Daniel see their dad one last time before he was taken to the funeral home. I wanted their final memory of John to be in our home, not laid out in a casket; there are some images that can never be erased from the mind. After saying their tearful goodbyes, Alyssa and Kevin returned to their house, and I called the funeral home to report that John had died. Within the hour, two representatives arrived in an unmarked van and carried John out on a stretcher. Daniel and I stayed in a back room. I could not bear to watch my life partner and best friend leave the house—forever. Once we heard the door close, we broke down. It was over. A delivery worker was sent to disassemble and remove the hospital bed and table. Daniel and I put the living room furniture back, and I thought, *What the hell actually ensued over the past six months?*

It was time to put the funeral arrangements in place: notify everyone of John's death, write his obituary, plan the visitation and memorial service—which included choosing music, flowers, photos, and coordinating the reception—and prep for out-of-town family members who would be staying with me. All the to-dos following a death are extremely trying and overwhelming, especially at an emotional time. While discussing the memorial service plans with Alyssa and Daniel, they indicated they wanted to say a few words. I considered speaking too, but it was definitely out of my comfort zone. However, I quickly realized the angst paled in comparison to what we had gone through. Alyssa, Daniel, and I drafted what we intended to say and asked the ministers overseeing the service to read our sentiments if we were unable to; we did not know what our emotional state would be.

When John was first diagnosed, he and I had a brief conversation about his funeral, especially when we were unsure if he would make it through the biopsy procedure. One essential idea John mentioned was that he wanted Daniel to play the guitar and sing "Falling Slowly," a song from the movie *Once*, which had a special place in John's heart. Daniel played this song at John's mother's memorial service years earlier. The music and lyrics are truly touching. When I told Daniel of his dad's wishes, he said he did not think he could do it. I told him I totally understood and asked him to think about it. After giving the idea a lot of thought, Daniel said he would try to play the song if he was in the right frame of mind.

Following John's death, the entrance to my home turned into a revolving door of out-of-town family members. Knowing I had family staying with me for a week, friends brought dinner and dropped off breakfast for the morning of the memorial service. I received a sliced ham from an out-of-town, long-time friend of John's who could not attend the services. These acts of kindness were so appreciated and lifted a weight off my shoulders.

The week was an extremely busy and mind-boggling seven days—a complete blur, to say the least. I knew what was involved in coordinating end-of-life arrangements after having gone through similar plans for my parents, but it took every ounce of strength I had to complete certain tasks for my husband's services. I had a hard time holding it together. Out-of-town relatives came and went depending on their schedules, leaving me often stressed, yet the support meant the world to me and overshadowed the anguish. Even though my children and I had six months to prepare ourselves for John's death, I quickly realized no one is ever actually prepared when a loved one passes away. There was no trying to make sense of the past six months. John's fateful diagnosis was so unexpected. My family and I were emotionally heartbroken, devastated, and numb. My boat, now without John, was slowly drifting in an unknown direction on the other side of a horrific storm.

The visitation gathering was surreal. My family and I arrived at the funeral home early. We set out selected photos of John's life, organized floral arrangements, and restlessly waited for the visitors to arrive. There were several unforeseen instances that took me by surprise—which will remain private—but I took them in stride and got through them. Although John was the only reason we were gathering, I could not believe my children and I played the main roles in this event. The turnout of guests was truly touching and humbling. People from all walks of life came to express sympathy, and their presence gave us much strength. The visitation was an emotional two-and-a-half hours, for which I believe no family is ever prepared. It was a somber, dreamlike, and hectic occasion, and in retrospect, I wish I had more time to speak with the visitors.

On the morning of the memorial service, we had quiches and fresh fruit from friends who delivered these items the previous day. I greatly appreciated these breakfast items as it undeniably lightened my load. The ministers leading the church service were prepared to read our eulogies, and if Daniel did not get up to play "Falling Slowly," they would skip to the next part of the service. Surprisingly, we were all able to speak, and Daniel performed the song. I felt much solace in how we honored John's life; he would have loved the service.

A reception followed, and I was surprised and emotionally moved by the number of people—local, in-state, and out-of-state—who attended, from family members, friends, and coworkers to business associates, neighbors, acquaintances, and fellow church members.

A private graveside service was held that afternoon for the immediate family. When our family returned home, I could not grasp what had transpired over the past six months. The day was draining and surreal. I had just buried and said my final goodbyes to my life partner and best friend. I do not even remember driving to the memorial service or parking my car at the church. I cannot even remember who was in the car with me. Looking back, I realize how glossed over and distraught my thinking was, and I knew the thirty-five-year chapter of my life had come to an end.

Christmas that year was unbearable. I had not done any shopping—no holiday spirit with my husband lying on his deathbed. I hastily and thoughtlessly shopped for my children and grandson, wanting them to have something to open on Christmas morning. I did what I could to make it endurable for my family, yet tremendous grief took its toll on us.

During the six months John was ill, I marveled at his courage to remain upbeat and positive. He and I always had fun together, even during the worst time in our lives. We had laughter and wonderful shared thoughts and moments, which hold a special place in my heart, but also a lot of distasteful, tough instances and situations. Hopefully, these difficult times will fade in my mind as time goes on.

John and I had often reflected during our years together that we had not experienced a lot of tragedy in our lives or the lives of our family. We always felt like we were living charmed lives, and we didn't take our blessings for granted. Yes, it was difficult when our parents, relatives, or dear friends passed away from health issues; no one is ever prepared to lose a loved one. John's unforeseen diagnosis and ultimate death show that you never know what is around the corner. Life can change in a split second. Every day is a gift; be thankful for each one.

I am determined not to let John's death pull me down—still. Death is a part of life. I am extremely grateful to have been happily married for almost thirty-five years, short by just two weeks. I will not throw myself a pity party. As hard as it has been, I find comfort in knowing how lucky I was to have had a wonderful husband who was also my best friend and a loving father to our children. I know I was truly blessed, and I deeply hold onto those core feelings, which gives me much comfort. There are hints of blue skies ahead of me, but they seem beyond the horizon. Amid my sorrow, I am adamant about being open to what may lie ahead. I know I will be okay, but it does not make getting through some days any easier. The world stops for a short time when someone passes away, then starts up again and keeps moving, but not for those who mourn the loss of someone special. That pain is deep.

I never expected or planned to write a book, but after a challenging and unbearable life-changing period, I felt called to write this resource. I am extremely passionate about the importance of reaching out to those dealing with a crisis. No one is immune to heartache, trauma, or death. Family and friends want to offer comfort and support but can often be hesitant or unsure how to proceed. I have firsthand experience and an understanding of what may be helpful after living through a devastating time. I have learned a lot since John's diagnosis and death and am adamant about paying it forward.

I cannot thank the caring people who supported me and stood by me through six months of pure hell and those who continue to hold my hand and be by my side many years later. They are true angels. I am grateful for their support, kindness, and friendship.

PART 2

Afterthoughts

I always thought of myself as emotionally grounded, experiencing life's ups and downs like anyone, always viewing my glass as half full. John's unexpected diagnosis and death put me in a full-scale tailspin for which I was totally unprepared to accept. My glass half-full was knocked over and shattered into a million pieces of emotional heartache and pain.

Growing up, I experienced occasional losses. The death of a few of my peers, brother-in-law, aunts, uncles, grandparents, parents' friends, parents, and in-laws left me brokenhearted. When my parents passed away—six weeks apart—when I was forty-five, I truly felt like an adult. It was a strange, empty feeling to be at the top of the chain. I felt very alone. Yes, I had my husband, children, and other family members by my side, but there was a hollow void and sorrow in losing my parents in such a short time. Mom and dad had been a part of my life for forty-five years, and within six weeks, they were gone. Fortunately, they never experienced major health problems or long, difficult illnesses. Both had medical concerns over the years, but the issues were treatable and managed until the last few weeks of their lives. My parents lived 2,200 miles away, so I was not always able to be with them or provide hands-on support. Thankfully, I was nearby when they passed away, and I found much comfort in being close when their lives abruptly ended.

While loading groceries into the trunk of her car, Mom fell in a parking lot, breaking her hip. Her health rapidly declined while she was in the hospital recovering from hip surgery. Mom barely ate and would not even attempt to work with the physical therapists to regain her strength and mobility. The lack of motivation surprised Dad and me as Mom would be on me in a heartbeat if roles were reversed. Further tests revealed she had lung and colon cancer, unbeknownst to us. Mom passed away three weeks later. The cancer diagnosis and her sudden death came without any warning. My family was totally shocked and devastated when she passed away.

Dad was a kind, caring, and emotionally strong man. I had seen him shed tears only a few times when family members or dear friends died. When Mom passed away, Dad was inconsolable. Like many people, there were times when vulnerability took over, and Dad was not afraid to show his emotions. To see Dad, the rock of the family, so grief-stricken was heartbreaking, and I felt helpless. Mom and Dad had been married just six months shy of their sixtieth wedding anniversary.

Five weeks after Mom died, tests indicated that unless Dad received a heart valve replacement, he would probably only live six more months. Dad had heart issues for many years, which were treatable and manageable. The surgery was immediately scheduled. He made it through the procedure but never recovered due to other health complications. He passed away a week later. Nothing could have prepared me for Dad's death, which I witnessed firsthand. I believe there is some truth to the cliché, *He died of a broken heart.* I cannot imagine Dad going on without his wife of almost sixty years.

If I had to sum up in one word how I felt following John's death, the word *broken* seems fitting. Imagine a glassful of red wine accidentally dropping on a ceramic floor. The glass shatters into countless shards. Red wine splatters everywhere, small droplets and large puddles, with some droplets and puddles seeping into the grout, leaving behind permanent stains. Ardently, this is exactly how I felt. My life, as I had known it for thirty-five years, had been broken. There are many emotional shards and stains that will remain with me for the rest of my life. My family was absolutely shattered.

Death is a part of life, and we are all going to face the death of family members, partners, friends, or, worst of all to me, a child. I am thankful I had my parents in my life as long as I did. It was not until their deaths that I truly understood that no one is ever prepared to lose a loved one. Over the years, I remember hearing people recall experiencing a broken heart, but I truly did not comprehend that a broken heart is an actual physical state of sorrow. Twice in my life, I have experienced the actual heaviness of a broken heart. The first time was many years ago, and the second time was when John died. There are truly no suitable words to describe the feeling of a broken heart; it is a real physical weight that may only be felt once or twice in someone's life.

Dealing with John's diagnosis and death just plain sucked (I can hear my mother's voice scolding me for using this word, but there is no other befitting term to describe that period). My life with John was comprised of a predetermined deck of playing cards, shuffled umpteen times, and when he was diagnosed with brain cancer, I had no choice but to play fifty-two card pickup.

I could not believe I was a widow at fifty-nine. I often reflect on our wedding vows, said in December 1980, never imagining he would pull the *in sickness and in health* card, ending with his final hand—*until death do us part*. How did thirty-five years of marriage go by in the blink of an eye? I imagined we would grow old together and move to a retirement community or health-care facility. I knew one of us would have health issues at some point in our lives. I am not so naïve to think nothing awful would happen, but nothing could have prepared me for his cancer diagnosis and death.

Our lives were changed forever the minute the neurosurgeon confirmed John had brain cancer. We were thrust into an unforeseen and extremely stressful time for which I was blindly navigating. Being John's sole caregiver twenty-four hours a day, seven days a week, for six months, was the most difficult thing I have ever endured. No matter how much I accomplished or stayed on top of things, I often hit snags that would pull me back into an unsettling state. I was extremely vulnerable. There was no light in sight in a dark tunnel of despair. I had no choice but to rally forward in whatever came into our paths. Unpredictability hovered over us; I was drowning in heartache. When the decision was made to put John into an at-home hospice program, helplessness and anxiety hit an all-time high.

As I said, John's only wishes were to see our first grandchild, know that Daniel completed his college degrees, and turn sixty-two. He lived to mark these important life events, which brings me much comfort. John passed away peacefully, which is not always the case with the terminally ill. Despite his general discomfort, surprisingly, he never experienced headaches or pain during the twelve to eighteen months he lived with brain cancer. I believe he is at peace. I have said many times to myself and my friends that I am not going to feel sorry for myself that my husband died and I am alone. However, I am honest enough with my emotions to admit I feel sorry for myself now and then, but I try not to dwell on it. Our marriage wasn't perfect, but we were happy, and we always had fun together.

John was a truly remarkable and relatable person. His infectious smile, genuine kindness, positivity, easy-going, fun personality, and sincereness to reach out to others are a testament to how he lived his life. He was a deep thinker and a people person, someone who never met a stranger. I admired his ability to connect with all people and maintain and nurture those bonds through the years, which came naturally to him. The relationships John formed with his friends, business associates, and colleagues were close and deep. John was one of the few individuals I knew who absolutely loved his career. When Sunday nights rolled around, he could not wait to go to work the next morning. He never considered work a job. How many people can honestly say that?

One thing John instilled in me and our children was to live life to the fullest. He often said, "You won't remember what you had for dinner last Wednesday night, but you will clearly recall meaningful moments and experiences." His life was rich and complete, and I know he felt blessed. Although our time together was cut short,

I treasure the time I had with him, and I will always have the wonderful memories from our forty-one years together. Recognizing how fortunate and privileged I am to have been John's wife, partner, and best friend helps me put one foot in front of the other and get through each day. I am a better person having known him.

Not long after John passed away, I felt like my life was over. The chapters of our life story had come to an end. I had a new, unwanted blank page of life staring at me. The fear of the uncertain path ahead was and continues to be incomprehensible. I felt and still feel alone and isolated. I was one of very few in my social circle who had lost a spouse, and I did not know what to do, where to turn, or who to talk to. I see that grief is the most mournful and loneliest road anyone will ever travel.

Following John's death, a handful of family and friends continually reached out to me, offering comfort and a shoulder to lean and cry on. The raw, emotional baggage I unloaded was heavy, and their sympathetic ears were immeasurable. They stood by me and listened while I wandered down a foreign path. I am grateful for their friendship and loyalty, and my heart is full when I think of their support during the darkest phase of my life. It's at your most difficult and challenging times when you discover who your true friends are. Some family and friends were there for me, and others turned their backs on me, maybe not on purpose, but they just weren't there.

I have had more than enough time to reflect on myself, relationships, and life in the last several years. I have discovered more about myself since John's death than in my entire life. I always felt reasonably emotionally grounded, yet I am surprised by how much his illness and death affected me as a person and how I view others. Although I am pretty much the same person as before, that period impacted me and reshaped who I am. I do not believe anyone remains the same after going through a devastating time. It leaves a permanent mark on you. I am good at appearing okay. I may look all right on the outside, but even after eight years, I still have raw, invisible wounds and continue to struggle to find my place in the world. When grief unexpectedly knocks on your front door, do you squint through the tiny peephole and hesitantly crack the door ajar or cautiously open it and let the uninvited dark emotions inside? The mysteries of life seem questionable now. I have many layers of emotions that I have never experienced, which I continue to process.

I always thought I had a realistic perspective about what matters. In retrospect, I see I had fallen short on that notion. During a tragic time, especially when it ends in death, *perspective* undeniably has a different meaning. I have always been a busy, active person, and I know how easy it is to lose sight of what's important. I am sad to admit that it took John's death for me to see life clearer. My outlook on what matters and what is meaningful has changed and is more pronounced. I have a renewed view of the world and appreciate life's wonders and gifts. I understand *the game of life* more and treasure and value family, friends, relationships, and experiences.

Living in the moment also has a new meaning. Today, I am intentionally thoughtful and mindful, and I listen more. I understand the importance of faithfully reaching out to others and genuine acts of kindness in good times and sad times.

"Don't sweat the small stuff," no matter the situation or predicament, was a common one-liner by John's father. It is natural to be annoyed by bumper-to-bumper traffic, the plumber who never shows up to repair a broken pipe, or the doctor running behind with appointments. That being said, sweating the small stuff pales in comparison to enduring a tragedy. I am sure my deceased father-in-law is smiling down on me. His words continue to play on repeat in my mind.

Even though I had six months to process John's diagnosis, the death of a spouse, expected or unexpected, is something no one can be prepared for. Unless someone has experienced it firsthand, it is impossible to imagine. I often wonder what is harder—losing a loved one suddenly, within a few months, or dealing with a lingering illness for many years. They are all different, but despite the circumstances, a loss is a loss, and the grief may be massive. And while my loss is gigantic, my children's loss of their father is totally different from me losing my partner.

I am more brokenhearted for my children than I am for myself. I am an adult, who, at fifty-nine, had seen and experienced hardships and losses. As hard as it was for me, watching my children (twenty-nine and twenty-two when John died) grapple with the reality was emotionally painful. John was an amazing, caring, hands-on father who put our children first, carved out time for them, listened when they spoke, and passed on knowledge and advice. It was important to John to share trivial facts, deep thoughts, and life lessons, whether they listened or not. I am sad their time with him was cut short, and they will miss out on his love, support, guidance, and presence during relationships, higher education, careers, children, life-changing events, etc. I frequently remind Alyssa and Daniel to focus on how lucky they were to have had a wonderful dad and not fixate on their loss; easier said than done, right? But they're lucky to have had abundant memories that will forever be held close to their heart.

Once the funeral passed and my life settled down, John's death only then began to sink in. All our plans and dreams for the future were gone. I felt cheated. Cheated on the future I thought I would share with John. The rest of the world returned to normal, yet I was left with a thousand crushed emotions that could never be put back together. Although I had a future, I had no idea what it would entail. I had to rebuild my life. *How and where do I begin?*

Grieving is individual and personal, and the process should not be rushed. Healing takes time, and bereavement has no timeline. Grief stirs mixed emotions, from fear, pain, sadness, worry, confusion, and anxiety to despair, anger, and rage, not to mention confusing contradictory feelings. Grief is often categorized into the following stages (according to the Cleveland Clinic):

- Denial (difficulty accepting what occurred)
- Anger (why did this person have to die?)
- Bargaining (all the what-ifs, making deals and promises with God if you are religious)
- Depression (uncertainty, sadness, loneliness, etc.)
- Acceptance (accepting that the person died)

Survivors may experience one or more of these stages, and they might not occur in any specific order. I only fell into one area—acceptance. Acceptance does not mean I came to terms with John's death, but I realized we could not pull a rabbit out of a hat and magically change the outcome of his illness. I knew that John's diagnosis was a death sentence from day one; I just wasn't sure how long he would live and what that time would be like. Somehow, I had to dig deep to find any remnants of inner strength and faith while coping with crippling emotional pain and sorrow.

Guilt can also play a large part in the grieving process. Many survivors experience varied layers of guilt associated with all the questionable wonderings and what-ifs. What if denial clouded my thinking? What if an alternative treatment could have offered survival? Why didn't I see a problem? Should I have stepped in to help sooner? Could I have done something different to change the outcome? Words may have been left unsaid to the affected person or the person's family or friends who were deep in the trenches of the crisis. Anyone who has lost someone by suicide may experience endless controversial questions and carry guilt, regret, or remorse, which is understandable.

Soon after John's death, I heard from several friends that Alyssa and Daniel were worried about me. The funny thing was that I was concerned about them. So here we were, the three of us, terribly troubled for one another. Alyssa and Daniel were fearful of me living alone for the first time in thirty-five years. I worried about them lacking the emotional wherewithal to process his death and needing their dad in their lives. It was difficult to lose my parents when I was forty-five, so I could not imagine the depth of their loss.

A dear friend passed away at forty-six, leaving a husband and four children, ages eighteen to twenty-four. A neighbor passed away, leaving a husband and two boys, ages eight and eleven. My daughter knows a young woman whose husband died at thirty-four from the same type of brain cancer as John, leaving his wife, an eight-year-old daughter, and a newborn. When I think of these families, I have heartache for the children left behind, including my own.

The first year following John's death, my head was in a painful, thick, mournful fog. I was always the type to stay on top of everything—daily responsibilities, appointments, paperwork, family and friends' birthdays, personal and business issues, etc. However, I became absent-minded, forgetful of routine tasks. Menial undertakings felt overwhelming and exhausting; days seemed unmanageable. I recall doing errands and driving past the bank, even though it was the first stop on the agenda. One morning, I went into the alcove at the post office to check my mailbox and realized I was in the wrong spot when the key did not fit the box. Although my mind was not on John at the time, I was obviously unfocused. On several occasions, when I met with professionals to discuss personal and business matters, I saw their mouths move, but they might as well have been speaking another language. I quickly discovered that grief plays tricks on the mind. I needed to slow down, concentrate, and focus on the tasks at hand.

I found ordinary activities demanding and taxing. Not only was it hard to concentrate on normal projects, but all the to-dos following John's death added more weight to my emotional pain. Grief clouded my thinking and judgment regarding several business matters. After giving these issues thorough consideration, I felt I was being taken advantage of by people who knew I was recently widowed; they were preying on my brittle vulnerability. As awkward as it was, I confronted the individuals, and things got back on track. However, this was a setback I did not need.

Most days, it was all I could do to get out of bed and face yet another day with a bogus smile on my mournful face. I was falling apart with the loss of John. My spirit disappeared into a dismal, unexpected reality that I wasn't prepared to grasp or deal with. I cannot put into words how hard it was to put one foot in front of the other and get through some days, which, at times, felt impossible, and handle all the routine responsibilities along with grappling with the chain reaction of John's death. I felt like I was barely hanging on to life by a fine, twisted thread loosely wound around an almost empty spool of sorrow. I knew I had to pull myself up by the bootstraps, but I did not know how and often lacked the strength to do so.

At times, it was hard to be cheerful when my whole world had totally crumbled. The rippling effects of grief stirred many of my emotions, and I had no idea how to reconcile these distraught feelings. The shadow of grief can be massively dark, and although it may fade at times, it truly never disappears. When I would be having a good day, grief reversed me into a deep, sorrowful state. Without warning, something I heard, saw, or may have been doing unexpectedly hit an emotional nerve, and I was drawn back into profound mournfulness. It's hard not to cling to the past, but it's difficult to move forward. The white noise of grief would scream at me. Despite my efforts, my life was no longer normal. The puzzle pieces of my world were randomly scattered in an irregular pattern; many pieces will never connect again, and some pieces will be missing forever.

The only thing that helped me get out of bed in the morning was thinking about my children. What kind of message would it send to Alyssa and Daniel if I was still in bed at 11? I had to pull myself together for their sakes . . . and mine. I was not prepared to help them deal with the loss of their dad. It was difficult to set aside my heartache to help my children process their pain. I spent time trying to guide them on how to cope with their loss while pushing aside my grief. I hope Alyssa and Daniel learn that no matter what obstacles in life come into play, hardships cannot be brushed aside or ignored.

Many times, circumstances and predicaments are out of our control. I want my children to be resilient when things in life trip them up if, or when, they are thrown a devastating curve ball.

It is not unusual for widows and widowers to struggle with being alone. Nightfall seems to be the hardest time of the day. The solitude, emptiness, and quietness in the house can be thunderous. Fortunately, I am comfortable in my home, especially since John passed away in the house. I lived on my own before John and I were married, and I was always content by myself. John traveled a lot for business, so I was used to being alone, which helped. There is a vast difference between being alone and being lonely. Although I am now alone, I am rarely lonely.

Occasionally, I reflect on the people who attended John's visitation and memorial service. Once the funeral was over, everyone moved on with their lives, and the support dwindled. A handful of friends continued to reach out to me and were a huge support in getting me out of the house and back among the living. However, I had nothing to talk about. My whole world revolved around caring for John when he was sick and then processing the aftermath. It was a strange feeling to be unable to contribute to a conversation. For so long, I barely kept up with what was going on in the world, had not gone anywhere special, and had not done anything besides be a caregiver or mourn John's death.

The loss of John brings many thoughts and mixed emotions that pierce my heart:

- My everyday life—for almost thirty-five years (12,775 days)—was over.
- All the hopes, plans, and dreams John and I had for our future ended.
- Daily routines (enjoying a cup of coffee and the newspaper with John, sitting at the kitchen or dining room table, sharing our days, etc.) were gone.

- When dining with my children or friends, the empty chair at a table for four glares at me. I feel stabbed in the heart when the server asks, "Are you waiting for someone?"
- I feel like a third or fifth wheel when out with other couples.
- My role as Mom is now Mom with a little bit of Dad in me. I will never be able to take John's place, but I need to be present for my children now more than ever.
- It is no longer *Tish and John*—it's just *Tish*.
- It is strange to sign greeting and holiday cards *Tish* and not *Tish and John*.
- I want to share something John would find noteworthy or love to know, but he is not here.
- For half of my life, I bounced ideas off John, and I no longer have that special person to confide in or share thoughts, views, or stories with; this void is indescribable.

Soon after John died, I had time to schedule routine medical checkups. These appointments ranked low on my calendar when John was ill, as I needed to focus my attention on him. At the rescheduled exams, I was handed a clipboard with the standard medical forms and asked to return the paperwork to the receptionist once I updated the information. I just about broke down in tears when I got to the *marital status* and *emergency contact* sections. The change in marital status and contact information hit me harder than I expected. I just wanted to return the clipboard, go home, crawl into bed, and pull the covers over my head. It was hard to reconcile my new marital status—widow. *Who should I list as my emergency contact person?*

Months after John's death, the grave marker I ordered arrived, and I stopped by the cemetery to see it in place. It was haunting to see John's name, date of birth, and date of death etched on the marker—and even stranger to see my name and date of birth on the marker; the date of death is the only part missing. I mentioned to Alyssa and Daniel that the marker was in place, and Alyssa stopped by the cemetery to see it. She immediately called me, upset and adamant that the marker was in the wrong place. I told her that could not be, but I agreed to meet with the representative to take a closer look. Well, Alyssa was right. When I met with the cemetery spokesperson, it was discovered that the marker had been centered between John's grave and the neighboring plot. It was an easy fix for the cemetery to move the marker to the correct spot but an emotional pang we did not need. I am thankful this was discovered early and not years down the road.

One morning, I was at a craft store when it dawned on me to buy flowers for the marker vase. I purchased silk flowers for each season and a couple of holidays. It was a sickening feeling and surreal awakening when I got to the checkout counter that I was buying flowers for my husband's grave. Never in a million years did I imagine I would be visiting my husband's gravesite, let alone buying flowers for it.

I felt like I was carrying around a fifty-pound bag of grief for a whole year. Everywhere I went, everything I did, and everyone I was with, this bag weighed me down—getting up in the morning, answering the phone, dressing for work, attending an exercise class, making it to a club meeting, and attending a worship service. This heavy emotional load may not have been a topic of conversation when I was with others, but it was always silently testing me and gnawing at my spirit. I was gradually disappearing into a foggy haze of existence, completely lost in my world of sorrow. It took a year to realize I needed to let some of the weight go. I will never forget John, but what my family and I went through was in our past, and I knew it was not healthy to carry this heavy burden everywhere.

As the first-year milestone approached, uneasiness consumed me. Over the year, some days slowly dragged on while others passed quickly. John often remarked that he thought time was a funny thing. At times, months and years seem to fly by, and on occasions, time seems to idle. Time was playing tricks on me. I could not believe a year had passed since John died. Surprisingly, I got through the day feeling somewhat relieved that the first year was behind me. I understood that the tragic period was part of my past.

Following John's death, the world seemed to have gone silent, at least for me. Everyone returned to their daily routines, yet I was left alone, wrestling with the troubling emotions of grief. I felt deeply cemented in my emotions. I do not think trite sayings such as "move on" or "let things go" are the correct answers, if there are even any proven answers when attempting to process a death. The only words that seem to fit are "move forward." I needed to pull up my anchor, which kept me from edging ahead. Grieving is without a specific timeline. No one ever gets over losing someone special, but I feel certain emotions, and life will get easier. The mournful fog lifts a little bit as time passes.

Many of my brittle emotions were silently written down on several sheets of paper, one by one, page after page, each sheet carefully folded in half, then folded in half again, and stored in a small, private, locked box for safekeeping. It is painful to confront these feelings, so it's easier to keep them locked up—out of sight, out of mind. The reality of what my family and I went through is difficult to come to terms with, yet I know I must unlock the box and face what is inside. It is so hard. I know in my heart that I will be okay, but it does not make getting through some days any more doable.

I always considered myself empathetic and compassionate, trying my best to reach out and lend support to those struggling. Looking back, I am not sure I reached out enough or provided sufficient backing for those dealing with challenges. Following John's diagnosis and death, I am more intentionally thoughtful, mindful, and sensitive to others. I know firsthand how painful, crippling, and isolating hardship can be. No one should ever feel alone or forgotten.

Occasionally I think back to the month that John was in the rehab unit. For thirty straight days, I drove to the hospital, parked my car, grabbed my tote bag, and wound my way through the hallways.

Most days, I saw many of the same people in passing and nodded to them. It dawned on me one day that no one knows what's going on in someone's life or the depths of their troubles. It was a lightbulb moment, realizing others were dealing with worse problems and possibly for a longer period. Everyone has a story, a hidden journey (a crumbing relationship, single parenting, financial strains, health issues, mental illness, substance abuse, addictions, overdoses, abuse, problems with teenagers or family members, military deployment, job loss, homelessness, attempted suicide, grieving the death of a loved one, life-long difficulties, natural or worldwide disasters, etc.). I now have a deeper understanding of my empathy and compassion.

In my early twenties, I remember hearing if you can count on one hand the number of your genuine friends, you are extremely lucky. I had never forgotten this truism. I am a social person and value my friendships—a closeness and bond I truly treasure. I do not take these relationships lightly or for granted. Through texts, emails, calls, cards, or other kind actions, I felt loved, and their concern for my family was deeply touching and comforting. A handful of friends have patiently been there for me as I unloaded intimate, inner emotional baggage. They stood by me, held my hand, and continue to be by my side. I have told them that I am eternally grateful for their friendship and support, but words are not enough.

After John's diagnosis, I gave myself a limitless pass and took a leave of absence from my part-time job and dropped out of committees, groups, and clubs to focus on John and our bleak situation. We needed this time together. Never in thirty-four years of marriage did I feel more committed and devoted as a wife, partner, and best friend. My pass continues to this day, as I still have a lot of tangled emotions to work through. Time alone allows me to be, think, reflect, and process without outside distractions. Alone time does not mean I sit and dwell on the past, but it has helped me as I attempt to heal.

Not long after John's death, I searched for bereavement materials, books, support groups, etc., but I have yet to come across a helpful resource. Nothing can take away the heartache, pain, and void; no one can say or do anything to make those grieving feel better. The hole in my heart remains empty yet heavy. Even though my family and friends have been supportive, this is an unfamiliar journey I must face alone. I have a new road to travel as I traverse this sad ordeal and attempt to figure out what my new *new* may be. I also realized how much my roles defined me as a partner and mother.

No one is in complete control. Life happens. Things do not always work out as we anticipate or plan. The only constant in life is change. Even though I went through a tragic time, I will continue to appreciate my blessings. My faith, strength, and resilience have been tested. I have learned that God's timing is not always our timing. Some things are out of our control. Why do bad things happen to good people? If God is so great, why did this happen to my husband? I find it thought-provoking that many people turn to God when times are difficult, perhaps looking for something in return—healing, comfort, peace, security, or a miracle. What about when things in life are going well? Do we prayerfully appreciate when things are going well? Are we grateful for others' kindness and outreach when facing good times and bad? I am much more mindful of these questions today.

I believe everyone has a gift. When tragedy strikes, and support is needed, it is heartwarming how these gifts present themselves. Perhaps someone's gift is calling those going through a rough period just to talk, mailing a note of concern, dropping off a meal, offering child care, picking up items at the drug or grocery store, washing, drying, folding a load of laundry, doing housework, walking the dog, mowing the grass, or visiting someone going through treatment, who's homebound, or who's in the hospital. When we needed a wheelchair ramp at the house, my friend and her husband built a ramp with no questions asked. Other friends reached out through cards, food items, flowers, and unexpected gifts or a sympathetic ear during our trying time.

What baffled me the most was not hearing from some family members, friends, and neighbors, including people John and I frequently met for dinner, entertained in our home, knew from social groups, spent holidays with, traveled with, or provided meals and child care for, and yet they failed to reach out to me in any way. Some of these people were a significant part of my life and in the lives of my children. I have run into a few of them, and they cheerfully say hello and how good it is to see me, but they have never acknowledged my loss, mentioned John's name, or asked how the family is. Yes, I asked for privacy during John's illness, but following his death, there was not a need for it anymore, and this was the time I needed support more than ever. Many times, it was obvious when people were avoiding me. John did not stub his toe or have the flu—he died of a terminal illness. If John had broken his leg, I'm sure I would be asked how he was, if he had a cast on, and if he could drive. Why is death different?

The lack of acknowledging my loss is hurtful and disrespectful to me, my children, and John's memory. Their silence is blatant. The *elephant in the room* has been present on many occasions, leaving me perplexed and unhinged. I do not understand it. Not acknowledging our loss makes me feel like people have turned their backs on us. We went through months of pure hell. How can others act like it is just another day when they see me or my children? Are people too self-absorbed to show empathy or compassion? There are no words to describe how crushed and emotionally bruised I felt. Do others realize they will be in my shoes at some point? It is hard not to be bitter—hard not to let a lack of empathy and compassion wear me down.

A few months after John's death, I was with a group of people I've known for fifteen years. One person in the crowd asked how I was doing, to which I replied, "I'm hanging in there," which was my usual response. I was then asked how my daughter was doing. I responded, "She's having a tough time." The woman said, "Oh? Is she sick?" to which I answered, "Uh, no, she's not sick. Um . . . her father just died."

The person dismissed my response, stating, "Well, I don't think my kids would have a tough time if their father died." I was shocked and dumbfounded. I could not believe the insensitivity; clearly, she was clueless. Only one person in the group had acknowledged my loss, leaving me confused and puzzled by their lack of concern.

On another occasion, I was with a group of about forty individuals, most of whom I had known for more than twenty-five years. Of those forty people, only three acknowledged my loss; the others never uttered a word and acted like it was just another day.

I am part of another group that gets together several times a year, and most of those individuals have never addressed my heartbreak, leaving me bewildered. At several dinners with friends, John's name never came up. I was never asked how I was or how my children were coping. When rethinking the evening, I was dismayed and confused by the avoidance. Were these *friends* waiting for me to bring up my loss first, or have some people forgotten that my husband died and my children lost their father? The tragedy is silently front and center in my family's lives, from waking up until the sun sets—we carry it with us everywhere.

The sadness following any death seems to lessen as time goes on, but it truly never goes away. It is an emotional roller-coaster ride for which no one is ever primed. The topic of death is uncomfortable. I am not uneasy discussing John's death, but I do not bring it up with others or share my grief. I do not want anyone to feel uncomfortable, and honestly, no one wants to hear the tragic details. But it means the world when someone addresses John's death, shares a story, or recalls a particular incident about John, meaning he has not been forgotten.

Some people pride themselves on Miss Manners etiquette, and others are regular churchgoers who sit in their self-assigned pew every Sunday, never having acknowledged my pain. I believe people care, yet I can only assume they are unsure, awkward, or uneasy to address our heartbreaking time. If this is the case, how unbelievably sad. I considered these people friends. Obviously, I thought more of the bond than they did. It has ripped my heart out. On top of contending with my husband's death, I was reconciling fractured friendships. Death can change relationships. Are my expectations of others too high or self-imposed?

I am part of a group that frequently meets throughout the year. One person remarked that she felt under the weather and scheduled an appointment with her doctor to find out what may be going on. Within a couple of days, I circled back around to see how she was feeling and got an update. She filled me in on her appointment and, wanting privacy, asked me not to share the information with the others. I was troubled when I learned that no one else checked on her or connected with her. Did they not care? Could they not take a minute out of their day to consider someone who may be dealing with a health issue? I find this very disheartening. Where is the humanity, empathy, compassion, understanding, and kindness?

My children had similar experiences with friends. I can understand my children's friends not addressing their dad's passing, as most have not gone through a demise like that at their age, but I thought my peers would be a bit more perceptive. Several adults had been a part of my children's lives growing up, yet they have never acknowledged their dad's death or reached out to them (through a note, phone call, or speaking to them in person). *Are my expectations unrealistic?*

Soon after John's death, I was invited to several social gatherings, but I declined the invitations. As much as I appreciated the inclusion, my heart was not ready for lively get-togethers. No one can imagine how hard it is to attend a joyful function following the death of a spouse. After further efforts to encourage me to venture out, some people gave up. I completely understand why, but anyone suffering a loss has good and bad days and may not be up for a social gathering. I wish others understood that, at some point, I may be ready to accept their invitations.

I heard through the grapevine that some friends wanted to give me space to process what I went through. There is no tried-and-true guidebook for processing grief. No one should assume that someone wants to be left alone unless the hurting person specifically says he or she needs some space. Outsiders need to understand that the waves of crippling emotions can be rough, rocky, and unsettling. Feelings of uneasiness and the lack of empathy and compassion on the part of others needs to change.

Several years ago, I watched a television documentary on the 2012 Sandy Hook Elementary School shootings in Connecticut. As I listened to a parent discuss how she was coping following the senseless shooting of her child, the mother had the same feelings about acknowledgment and compassion from others. People she ran into never addressed the incident or mentioned her child's name, who was killed, carrying on as if it was just another day. The lack of acknowledgment made her feel like her child never mattered or even existed.

I am aware of several people who were upset that they were not able to stop by to see John in the last few months of his life. I understand how others may have felt when I turned down their request for a visit, but my top priority was caring for John, and visitors were the last thing I could think about. Our days were incredibly full, long, and stressful. There was rarely a day that I could even consider someone stopping by even for a few minutes. Unless you have cared for a terminally ill person, you cannot even imagine how difficult and heart-wrenching it is. I feel these individuals were selfish, not fully giving consideration to our tragic situation and our need for privacy.

On several occasions, when John was at home in hospice and following his death, my doorbell rang at inopportune times. My children and I weren't up for greeting anyone, regardless of who it was. I later learned that these visitors were offended that we did not come to the door, aware that we were at home. It's hurtful knowing they were clearly troubled, putting an uncalled-for burden back on us when we just wanted a little solitude as we were grieving. I do not understand why others could not have empathy and realize we were not up for company.

Death can change associations for many reasons, which is unfortunate. I consider a healthy relationship one of mutual respect, concern, support, and being there when someone needs it. John's diagnosis and death have driven me to reevaluate some connections and friendships. I am more guarded and feel uncomfortable in a large group setting. I have had to distance myself and sever ties with several people to maintain a secure frame of mind. Perhaps the association was never truly genuine, or the relationship was already fractured, and a traumatic ordeal or death was the final straw that ended the connection. It has been over eight years since John died, and I still feel uneasy around those who have never acknowledged my loss or reached out, people I considered friends. Their silence is hurtful. Having a compassionate heart can be troubling because you expect everyone to care as much as you . . . and they don't.

During John's illness, some people were front and center from day one. They reached out and generally checked on us from time to time. Following his death, I have not heard a thing from most of them. I do not understand it. It is like they have fallen off the face of the earth, or perhaps, have I? On the flip side, unexpected friends have reached out to me, and my heart is very grateful and full for their kindness and moral support. Most of the individuals who have continued to touch base with me have never endured or come close to experiencing what I have, yet they have been thoughtful and supportive. They cared enough to regularly check in with me, listened when I needed a sympathetic ear, and were there during and after our heartbreaking time. Why do they get it and others do not? Hard times reveal authentic relationships.

Several people have mentioned that "Susie" asked about me and has not reached out because she doesn't know what to say. Really? Why are people so uneasy about addressing another's hardship? Most people genuinely care when a relative, friend, acquaintance, or coworker experiences a tragic time, yet certain situations or deaths can feel awkward and uncomfortable. Some painful ordeals can be foreign, tragic, and/or horrific, and death is just as tenuous and heavy. People don't know what to say, are afraid of saying the wrong thing, or feel they'll increase my sadness by bringing me to tears. When people see me with a smile on my face, which is often forced, they may not want to bring up John's name. Troubling times are uncomfortable, but quite frankly, it is not about them; it is about my family. Acknowledging John and our tragedy gives us more strength than anyone can imagine.

Alyssa was settled in her career, married, and expecting her first child when John was diagnosed. She and her dad had an extraordinary relationship. They talked on the phone almost every morning while Alyssa made her forty-minute commute to work. John planned father-daughter dinners several times a year—a special time without distractions to enjoy a meal and connect one-on-one. Alyssa and her husband were excited about the arrival of their baby. John was able to meet our first grandchild, Wyatt, and we were thrilled to be grandparents. Gone are the phone calls and special dinners. John's absence is enormous. He would be proud of the wonderful mother Alyssa is and her commitment to her family, career, and volunteer work.

John and Daniel had a wonderful father-son connection. John spent a lot of one-on-one time with Daniel, focusing on deep conversation, shared interests, and traveling together. They made unforgettable, lasting memories. Daniel's help and support at home were immeasurable during John's illness. After John died, Daniel applied for a job in another state, and after several interviews, he was offered the position. As much as I hated to see Daniel leave, he needed a fresh start. Daniel loved his new job, and he feels blessed to work in a field that is important and meaningful to him. Five and a half years later, Daniel took a position in his hometown, and he felt fortunate and enthusiastic about the career opportunity. He has had to grow up faster than most. John would be so proud of Daniel and his passion and commitment to his profession.

Not a day goes by that we do not think of John. Some days are better than others. Everything has changed, from daily routines, family meals, birthdays, and holidays to cookouts and vacations. We make a concerted effort to do new and different things so the void is a little more manageable. We need to learn to live without John, but the emptiness is massive. His death has shattered our family beyond words. We have no choice but to live with his absence.

Yes, life can be tough. Yes, life can be unfair. But I am determined not to let John's death pull me down. I know I can accomplish anything I set my mind to or deal with situations I may be up against. I have learned how resilient I am, which is good but a reflex I would have rather not discovered. I know I will be okay as time goes on, but it does not make some days any easier. Occasionally, my eyes well up as I go about my daily routine and a thought or memory comes to mind. I wake up every morning, and it is up to me to decide what kind of day I will have; I can *choose* to make it a good day. I need to be okay so my children will be okay. I make a deliberate attempt to keep my days chock-full; perhaps I am trying to outrun the grief. I stay busy and do at least one productive thing each day—handling paperwork, working in the yard, cleaning out a closet, etc., so I know I have done something worthwhile. Everything is different now. I must consciously work on being emotionally okay. I need to silence the grieving voices in my head to move forward. Baby steps are the best I can do, and that is okay. Every day is a gift.

I would not change a thing about how I dealt with John's health crisis. Each day went downhill, but I kept on as best I could. Looking back, though, I wish I had asked John certain questions or discussed specific topics with him, but that is in hindsight. We all experience it. Our days were so wrapped up with what was on our plate that I did not have the time to think about unanswered questions or discuss certain topics. Thankfully, this is the only regret I have.

Since I have more time to self-reflect, ponder connections, and speculate on life's true meaning, I have a different outlook on people, relationships, and life. Just like anyone else, I was guilty of taking each day for granted. It is not the big house, expensive car, or luxurious vacation that is important . . . it is people and our relationships.

I have irrevocably changed. I am stronger and have grown in the last few years. Life has a different, more insightful meaning to me today. I listen closer. I am a better person and friend because of John's death. I have no doubt that any crisis can have enormous effects on us.

Dear friends' phrases have touched me, providing encouragement and support after John's death:

- Things do not get better, but they get easier.
- Honor how your husband lived rather than dwelling on his death.
- The deeper the grief, the more loved your husband was.
- Grief is just love with nowhere to go.
- Live the life you have; do not spend time thinking about what is missing.
- Remember that the love you had for your husband makes each day worth living because love never dies; you just need to direct it somewhere else.

What is next for me? I have no idea. My past is behind me. What I used to consider normal is now uncertain. I have joyous moments, but the pleasure of daily living escapes me. As I think about my future, one eye is always looking in the rearview mirror of my life.

Time passes. Seasons change. Years go by. Life goes on. I do not want to be left behind.

Life is for the living.

PART 3

Helping Others in Crisis

It is only natural for people to get wrapped up in the busyness of daily life associated with family, friends, work, everyday demands, and all the *to dos* that need to be accomplished. At the same time, we all need to be reminded to be thankful and appreciate the blessings in our lives even when experiencing challenging times. It is understandably hard to be grateful when something goes awry and our world shifts, crumbles, or falls apart. Life can change in a split second, altering a planned path. When a crisis occurs, outsiders are often hesitant, unsure, or puzzled about how to proceed. Situations may require hands-on support, perhaps the need to step back from family, friends, or groups, or simply a nonjudgmental ear to hear their concerns. Shouldn't we all show up and serve one another in good *and* difficult times?

There are no well-established or proven guidelines when someone is battling hardship. We all need to practice goodwill and kindness and do better in reaching out and responding to those struggling. It is crucial to be present for those facing an uncertain crossroad and lift them up with caring gestures, words of encouragement, and compassion; support is critical. Life can often get in the way when you want to lend assistance and your daily responsibilities are already demanding, your calendar is completely full, an unplanned work-related trip requires you to be out of town, etc. It is important to reach out when you are able—tomorrow, next week, next month, or even later. Your efforts will be appreciated.

Those in crisis may face emotional, physical, and financial strains. Anyone enduring a troubling circumstance may be up against a stressful, challenging, or life-changing situation, and a support system is essential. Those struggling may feel alone, on edge, stretched thin, or isolated. Some people may *check out* by brushing aside or ignoring the problem. Perhaps they have reached their tipping point, silently crying for help, and outsiders may not be aware of their worries. Oftentimes, those suffering or hurting may be in such a deep, dark hole, they may not have the ability or strength to pull themselves up or may possibly lack the courage or energy to ask for assistance. A tumultuous period can be debilitating during any challenging ordeal.

There is no question that you or someone you know will face a crisis at some point in life. A tumultuous hardship may not occur next week, next month, next year, or in the next few years, but no one is immune to challenges. Put yourself in someone else's shoes. No one should silently suffer or struggle. Ignoring another's predicament is unjustifiable. What can you do to ease someone's burdens? Can you shine a light on someone's darkness?

This section is meant to open the door for those on the outside of hardship on ways to reach out, respond, and support those in need without expecting accolades or anything in return. We are all human and can easily fall short of being kind, offering help to those struggling, and thinking outside of ourselves. Situations may be awkward, uncomfortable, or foreign, but there is no excuse for being a bystander to someone's troubles. Being front and center can be key. It is the little things that brighten someone's day and lessen stress and uncertainties.

It is my goal to present simple, practical ways to reach out without being too forward, pushy, overbearing, or intrusive. Having dealt with a devastating medical diagnosis that ended in the death of my husband, John, from inoperable brain cancer, many of the suggestions are a result of what helped my family as we encountered an unanticipated, fatal health nightmare that snowballed into six long, heartbreaking, stressful months. After living through a traumatic period, I am passionate about the importance of reaching out and responding to those dealing with a hardship because of my own experience and emotions from others who faced difficult adversities.

The suggestions can be tailored to your situation—depression, dementia, mental health issues, the uncertainty of medical tests, hospitalization, inpatient or outpatient surgery, miscarriage, occupational or physical therapy, rehabilitation, chemotherapy, troubled children, aging relatives, moving to an assisted living/nursing home, being homebound, emotional or physical abuse, addictions, overdose, attempted suicide, crumbling relationship, separation, divorce, disability, job loss, financial strain, hospice, death, incarceration, homelessness, home emergencies, natural disasters, etc.

Simple acts of kindness can come in unexpected ways. Support can be multifaceted. Actions frequently speak louder than words. No one truly knows what someone may be up against or going through. Everyone has a story—a personal journey. Just knowing others are thinking of those struggling can mean a lot. What can you do to bring sunshine to someone's cloudy day?

It is important to offer support where you feel most comfortable. For example, if you do not cook, providing a home-cooked meal may not be the best area to lend support, yet there are other ways you can extend a helping hand. Perhaps you can pick up a prepared meal from the grocery store or a restaurant. If you feel uncomfortable visiting someone in a hospital setting or a treatment facility, dropping a thinking-of-you note in the mail may be a better alternative. If you live a busy life and do not have a lot of spare time, purchasing a gift card and delivering it is a wonderful way to lend assistance. There is always some way you can lend support that suits your schedule or in an area you are most comfortable handling.

Personally, I get more satisfaction from helping others than being the recipient. It is rewarding to lessen another's weighty load and worries. It warms my heart to lend assistance, and I know my efforts are appreciated.

It is important to understand that everyone handles situations differently. Do not feel unsettled or put off if you reach out to those struggling and do not get a response. They may be overwhelmed or stumbling through a rough, dark spot. Circumstances and emotions often come in ominous waves. The lack of response should not stop you from reaching out again and again. You never know what others may be going through, and it is imperative to be sensitive to the troubles someone may be encountering.

Understanding Emotions

*Tragic events put everyday life in perspective.
Our time in the here and now is short and precious.*

Empathy and Compassion

Everyone will face a battle or crisis at some point in life, and if they are fortunate, the challenges will be few and minor. When a tumultuous time occurs, outreach from others may be the crucial element needed for those currently in the middle of a hardship to get through a rough period and/or attempt to move in a more positive direction. It can be difficult to put yourself in someone else's shoes when the situation or adversity may be bleak, foreign, unimaginable, unthinkable, and/or horrific. However, most people can *imagine* how it may feel to be in a similar circumstance. In other words, consider how you might feel and what would help you if you were dealing with a comparable ordeal.

It is important to not shy away during stormy times; those enduring challenges need empathy and compassion and may turn to others for emotional and physical support, keep everyone at arm's length, or withdraw from communication or assistance. Outsiders may have absolutely no clue of the emotional, physical, or financial toll someone may be experiencing. The *elephant in the room* occurs too many times and is frankly inexcusable if you are aware of someone's trying period. Too often, those well-intentioned sidestep a troubling time, perhaps feeling hesitant to come forward, uncertain how to help, or fear of saying or doing the wrong thing, but remaining silent or absent can be very hurtful and unsettling. Those suffering may assume others did not care when they remained speechless or disappeared, leaving the recipient puzzled or possibly feeling abandoned and perhaps resentful by the lack of others not reaching out. Approach someone's concerns head-on and acknowledge the distressing period. Those affected may be on shaky ground, wrestling with the problematic feelings of a particular circumstance or predicament, or possibly cemented in the crosscurrent of a situation, unable to see any way out. There may not be a cure to a medical issue or an answer to a troubling circumstance, making it difficult for those in turmoil to hold on to any inkling of hope. Emotions may range from feeling apprehensive, disillusioned, and/or scared to worried, depressed, stuck, and/or hitting rock bottom.

I will say this often in the book because it is so true: it's at troubling times when people need support from others the most. Do not assume to know or even begin to understand what others are facing, going through, or have endured. Show up, be present, listen, practice selfless acts of kindness, respond with generosity, address the tumultuous situation, consider others' needs, be encouraging, lend assistance, and do not disregard someone's feelings or be judgmental. Do not be a spectator by remaining silent or distant when someone's troubles are apparent and painful. What can you do to respond to another's difficulties or suffering?

Reach out.

Be Sensitive

The burdens that some people carry can be heavy, intense, complicated, overwhelming, or ominous. You may be standing in line at a fast-food restaurant, ready to place your order, waiting your turn in the checkout line at the local bookstore, filling up the car with gas, dining in a popular restaurant, or nodding a quick *hi* to those in your weekly exercise class, unaware of the toils or worries the person, couple, or family may be experiencing. Someone may be doubting hope, a cure, or a resolution of a particular circumstance, trusting those who have offered help, questioning his or her faith, searching for answers, or unable to see how he or she will even get through the day, let alone tomorrow or the day after that. Often, nonobvious circumstances or problems can pull someone's life down even though they appear to look all right on the outside. Be sensitive to those struggling who may need to step back from certain duties, get-togethers, committees, groups, events, large gatherings, etc., to deal with their troubles and perhaps get a better handle on the predicament.

For some, it is difficult to be positive; being hopeful or upbeat may feel impossible. Be mindful that those struggling may be barely getting through the day, ready to fall apart or collapse at any given moment, and may be barely balancing home life and/or workdays with their hardship. Some people may be stuck in a perplexing mindset, or their feelings may be so brittle, fragile, or bottled up that they cannot even begin to see how they are going to get through the day. They may be in survival mode, questioning the uncertain path of the twisty road ahead. Ordinary routines may feel consuming and unmanageable. Outsiders are often unaware of the gray depths of another's challenges or emotional state. It is a given that everyone will face a snag, scuffle, or blockade at some point in life or be on the receiving end of a conflict. Step outside of yourself; put yourself in someone else's shoes. Be sensitive to the distressing time another may be enduring.

Careful attention to mental health should be at the forefront of the predicament. Stress, anxiety, frustration, and uncertainties may be intense for those centered in crisis. People's lives may be on autopilot or an indefinite hiatus when life shifts, changes develop, or setbacks occur, which may be linked to daily struggles or unforeseen obstacles that arise. Family members and friends may be on different pages and/or split with which approach may be best to move in a more positive direction, such as medical treatments, living arrangements, financial troubles, etc., adding angst to an already stressful situation.

Be sensitive and speak cautiously when addressing another's stormy period. Words can have an extraordinary impact and lasting effect. Choose your words carefully to avoid conversations that might be upsetting or hurtful even though your intentions are made in good faith. Those hurting need kind words of concern, beneficial support, and heartfelt empathy.

Be respectful of others' wishes or boundaries. Everyone is unique. What may work for one person or family may not work for another, such as the need for meals, errands, child or pet care, laundry, etc. Some people are open and want to share their trying times with the world. Being open and forthcoming makes it easy for outsiders to connect and provide needed assistance. Others may prefer to preserve their privacy. It can be difficult to help those who want to keep their ordeal private, but their wishes should be honored. Reaching out to those in need is important whether they are open or closed in their circumstance. There is a fine line between being helpful and intrusive. What matters is that they know you are there for them.

It is important to never minimize pain or be judgmental. Realize that no one can fix another's difficulties, yet being supportive helps more than you know. Frequently, everyone involved is powerless. What would help you if you were in the same or a similar situation? Most people would appreciate receiving unbiased emotional and physical support.

Be mindful of anyone struggling who may be single, without adult children, or away from relatives. They may not have a solid anchor and truly appreciate assistance.

If someone entrusts you with private information, honor their wishes. You may feel the need to let others in on the circumstance, but it can be very hurtful and damaging. Keeping quiet includes not sharing with your spouse or close friends. Confidential means just that—confidential. Someone's story is theirs to share if and when they are ready.

Reach out.

A Pass

There may be times when those suffering need a break or an infinite pass to withdraw, regroup, or spend time away to deal with the troubling occurrence. Someone may need to step back or completely drop out of a committee, group, class, organization, etc. They should not feel guilty if a deadline cannot be met, an appearance is missed, or phone calls and emails go unanswered. The trying time needs to be their top priority. No one knows the gravity of someone's struggles. If you are aware of another's adversity, grant them time away or an unlimited detour.

Reach out.

When Privacy Is Requested

Respect those who ask for privacy to contend with their hardship. Whether you are a family member, close friend, or acquaintance, no one truly knows what is occurring in someone's life. If privacy is requested, your relationship should be your guide as to whether you should reach out with a phone call, text, email, or an in-person visit. Do not heed the need for privacy, thinking someone wants to be left alone. Being *alone* does not imply *don't reach out*; privacy means *please don't bombard me with communications or show up unannounced.* It can be hard to know when to take a step back, but it is important to respect boundaries. Those suffering may need a little space to attempt to make sense of their situation.

Those seeking complete privacy may want to leave a note on their door stating the need for solitude. If you want to drop something off, leave what you brought outside and call, text, or email the recipient. The communication should be brief to comply with the need for a little space.

If you are aware of someone struggling, ignoring the situation is hurtful and, quite honestly, inexcusable. Just because someone asks for privacy does not mean you should shy away, remain silent, or vanish; there are ways to reach out without being intrusive. A simple thinking-of-you note is a touching gesture and always appropriate. You can write your contact information on the card, noting your availability to help. Your thoughtfulness will mean a lot, and the recipient will be touched and feel less alone. If the crisis continues for several months, and the need for privacy is still in place, continue to connect through notes, flowers, food, gift cards, etc.

Reach out.

The Gift of Time

Time is truly a gift and one that many people take for granted. We all have the same number of hours in a day, and depending on how the hours in the day are spent by working, parenting, family time, groups, exercising, hobbies, sleeping, etc., some people may have more time than others. Daily roadblocks can easily get in the way of reaching out or responding. You may wonder if your one-time help will be enough or really matter. It is important to offer help, and time plays a key part in the assistance you may be able to offer.

If you are unable to help someone due to financial limitations, there are many ways to lend support. Do not feel that you need to drop off a meal, a gift card, a plant, etc., if funds are a concern. The gift of time is as simple as picking up the phone and touching base, lending a nonjudgmental ear to another's worries, sending a note of concern, accompanying someone to a therapy session or medical appointment, sitting with an ill person so the caregiver can have a break, providing light housework, assisting in looking over and paying routine bills or insurance paperwork, walking the dog, watering plants, mowing the grass, helping with technology issues, etc. The gift of time is precious.

Reach out.

Helpful Suggestions of Support

*No one should ever feel alone, forgotten,
or fall through the cracks. Kindness matters.*

Keeping Everyone Informed

When a crisis surfaces, it can be difficult to keep everyone current on the situation. An internet site is a wonderful way to update loved ones and friends on specific needs such as meals, grocery shopping, errands, rides to appointments, etc. Some families create an online site for this purpose, and there are user-friendly websites that are easily accessible and simple to set up and navigate. If those struggling are overwhelmed with their situation, offering to create a site may be appreciated. Again, every family is individual, and their emotional and physical needs may be different.

I am a private person and preferred to occasionally send out group emails about John's condition. I sent about four or five mass emails during his illness. The first email reported John's initial diagnosis. I asked for privacy as our lives came to a devastating halt. The last thing we needed or wanted was our phone constantly ringing, having to respond to numerous correspondence, or receiving unexpected visitors. Being bombarded with multiple communications would have sent me over the edge. I was very protective of John, and it was important that our days run as smoothly and quietly as possible. Family and close friends occasionally texted or emailed me that they were thinking about us, asked if there was something we needed, or let me know they had dropped something off at our front door, which meant a lot. Their thoughtfulness and outreach gave me strength. I responded to the texts, calls, or emails when I was able.

Reach out.

Cards! Cards! Cards!

The impact of a simple note or greeting card can be immeasurable. What an easy way to acknowledge someone's struggles and possibly lift a cloudy day. Whether a note or card is left in the recipient's mailbox, at their front door, or sent through the mail, it is a sincere way to show you care and are thinking of the person and/or the family. Even if a card has a printed verse, take the time to add a handwritten note to make it more meaningful. You do not need to buy a printed greeting card; a blank note is perfectly fine. Be mindful of the correct spelling of the affected person's name (Caroline/Carolyn, Catherine/Katherine/Kathryn, Cathy/Kathy, Debbie/Debby, Kirsten/Kristen, Lara/Laura, Sally/Sallie, Sara/Sarah, Brian/Bryan, Darrell/Darryl, Jeff/Geoff, John/Jon, Stephen/Steven, Tom/Thom, etc.). Misspelling someone's name lowers the intention of the note.

It can be hard to know what to write in a card. Here are some suggestions:

- *Please know that you and your family are in my thoughts and prayers at this difficult time.*
- *I was sad to learn of your recent diagnosis. Please know that I am thinking of you.*
- *I am here for you—don't hesitate to call on me.* Provide your contact information.

If you are part of a group, perhaps you and the others can jointly sign a thinking-of-you or get-well card. Combining the outreach will be appreciated.

Remember the caregiver. Caregivers carry a huge emotional

and physical weight and are often overwhelmed and stressed; they can be overlooked and even forgotten. The sacrifices they make are enormous. A separate card to acknowledge them may brighten a long, taxing day.

Many days, our mailbox was filled with cards addressed to John. John's face would light up when I handed him the countless notes he received; he was often brought to tears. Several times, he said, "I can't believe I'm getting all these messages of well-wishes." One business associate of John's sent him six or seven cards during his illness, and seeing the warmth on John's face showed me how powerful a note or card can be. Her handwritten messages were short and sweet and simply conveyed that she was thinking of him. The notes and cards I received made me feel a little less alone and gave my children and me added strength when attempting to quash challenges. Knowing others are thinking of those in the thick of a trying period cannot be measured, and this form of support meant a lot to my family and me.

Many years ago, a dear friend was terminally ill with cancer and eventually went into hospice. I was at a complete loss for how to support her and her family, especially since they lived in another state. After much thought, I decided to buy thinking-of-you cards, and every other day, I mailed her a note with a personal message, special memory, or detailed comment about how much her friendship meant to me. My friend was nearing the end of her life, and even though she may not have been able to read them, I believed it gave her family something to focus on. "Oh . . . you got another card from Tish. She writes, do you remember when we—"A note or card is an easy, meaningful way to show you care.

Reach out.

Pick Up the Phone

One of the easiest ways to support someone is to pick up the phone to touch base and check in. There is no excuse in dodging, remaining silent, or disappearing when you are aware of someone's struggles.

If you reach the hurting person, simply state, "I heard you are going through a rough time. Is this a good time to talk?" You only need to convey that you have been thinking of them and you wanted to reach out. Most often, those affected will fill you in on the trying period if it is a convenient time to talk and if they wish to share any news. Offer support in whatever the suffering person may be up against. Depending on the circumstance, you may want to check in again in a couple of days or weeks to see if there is anything you can do.

If you are only able to leave a voice message, simply convey, "I understand you are going through a difficult time. I've been thinking about you. Please give me a call when you have a minute." If you do not hear from them, you may want to reach out again with a phone call or note expressing concern.

If the unfortunate period continues for several months or longer, it is important to maintain communications and not disappear. Fading away can leave those suffering feeling confused, isolated, and abandoned when any form of interaction stops.

Reach out.

Providing Meals

Meals can be a tremendous help for anyone going through a challenging period, whether it is an expected or unexpected circumstance, upcoming medical procedure, planned or unplanned inpatient or outpatient surgery, etc. The affected person's days may be busy and exhausting, and the last thing they want to think about is what to serve for dinner when mealtime rolls around. It is important to determine if meals would be welcomed. What works for one person or family may not work for another, and that's okay.

Meal teams or meal trains are a wonderful outreach to those experiencing hardship. Meal teams can be organized by family members, friends, neighbors, coworkers, church groups, book clubs, a neighborhood, exercise groups, etc. It is best to have an organizer to oversee the process. The organizer should contact the recipient to ascertain the specifics:

- how often meals are needed
- how many people a meal should serve
- any likes, dislikes, dietary restrictions, or allergies
- the time of day and the address of where meals should be delivered
- if a cooler is available so the family does not need to be disturbed
- any additional information that might be helpful for volunteers to know

Online meal signup sites are user-friendly and make it easy. If space is available to note what you intend to bring on the day you volunteer to deliver a meal, add that comment (cobb salad, spaghetti, and meatballs; Caesar salad, chili, and cornbread; baked chicken and wild rice; pork tenderloin, potato casserole, etc.) for volunteers to view the main entrée others are bringing so that similar meals are not back-to-back. Be sure to follow the meal team instructions, which may specify food dislikes, allergies, or other important information.

When providing a meal, keep in mind the size of the family. If the person in need is single, provide a meal for two. In other words, do not bring a huge casserole. For a family of four, provide enough food plus a little extra. You do not want excess leftovers to be tossed, and the recipient may not have time or freezer space to portion out the meal for later. When making a meal that calls for a nine-by-thirteen-inch pan, you can easily divide the food into two eight-by-eight-inch pans, so the family can freeze one of the pans to heat later. A single person or caregiver would appreciate anything in single-serving containers that can be frozen and heated when needed.

If an individual or family requests privacy yet welcomes meals, a large cooler can be left at their front door for volunteers to drop off food without disturbing anyone. If the recipient does not have a large cooler, the organizer or another volunteer should provide one.

Meals delivered on Mondays and Thursdays or Mondays, Wednesdays, and Fridays seem to work well. The health of the ill person should also be your guide when providing a meal. Be mindful that even though there are no dietary restrictions, if someone has recently undergone surgery, a light diet is best, and rich and spicy foods should be avoided. Keep in mind that chemotherapy, radiation, and other medical treatments can affect a person's taste buds. Pregnant women or anyone receiving chemotherapy should avoid unwashed fruits and vegetables, soft cheeses, deli meats, and raw or undercooked meats. When preparing a meal for those immunocompromised, extra cleanliness precautions should be taken.

Items should be clearly labeled (lasagna, chicken, rice casserole, vegetable soup, green beans, chocolate pie, etc.), the name of the person who prepared the items, refrigerator, freezer, cooking, or reheating instructions, and the date. Food should be packaged in disposable containers. Do not use a container that needs to be returned or a breakable dish; those in crisis do not have the time to keep up with who brought what container or dish.

To keep food warm when transporting a meal, place a kitchen towel tightly over the pans until you arrive at the recipient's home. Simply remove the towel when you deliver the food. If you see the family, be sure to mention that you do not need any containers returned. A thoughtful gesture is to include paper plates and napkins to make serving and clean up effortless.

If you are uncertain if a cooler is available, it is easy to make your own *freezer pack*. Fill a quart-size or gallon-size bag with water, leaving about an inch or two of space at the top, squeezing out air before sealing the bag. Lay the bag flat in the freezer overnight, and you have an instant freezer pack that the family can dispose of. Inexpensive insulated shopping-size bags can be found at most grocery stores for a few dollars.

When I provide meals, I often bring extra items (quiche, croissants, bagels, muffins, fresh fruit, cold cuts, bread, soup, salad, a casserole, cookies, etc.). Additional food may not be needed in the next day or two, but I am sure it is appreciated down the road.

A thoughtful gesture is to reach out prior to drop-off to ask if they need anything you can pick up for them at the grocery store or drugstore. Since you are already slated to deliver a meal, dropping off needed items at the same time is easy and can lighten the recipient's load, such as a gallon of milk, a loaf of bread, juice, fruit, toiletries, paper products, etc.

If providing a meal by yourself seems a bit daunting, partner with a friend to make the task a bit more manageable. No one should feel obligated or pressured into making a homecooked meal, especially if you do not cook or enjoy cooking. Picking up a prepared meal from a grocery store or restaurant is fine. Pouring breakfast cereal into a bowl was the extent of my husband's cooking ability. However, he had a big heart and would be more than happy to deliver a prepared meal to anyone who needed it.

Be sensitive when dropping off food. The recipient may feel obliged to invite you in to chat for a bit; they may welcome a friendly face and a little light conversation other than dealing with their current difficulties. A short visit is fine, but the recipient doesn't need to entertain the one who brought dinner. Those enduring a trying time may have had a long, tiring day and just want to eat and settle in for the evening. Use your judgment and keep the visit brief.

Honor a family's wishes if they do not accept an organized meal team or food. I know several families who turned down the offer because of picky eaters or the need for privacy. Perhaps they do not want to be bombarded with numerous people bringing food, they may have finicky eaters, they may feel that meals are a burden for others to prepare and drop off, or they truly need privacy and do not want to be disturbed. Comply with boundaries. If you find this to be the case, a gift card to a local restaurant or grocery store is a wonderful alternative.

If you feel someone could use a meal even though the offer of a meal team was turned down, the best approach is to say, "I would like to bring you dinner next week. Does Tuesday or Thursday work for you?" When you are specific in what you are proposing, the recipient may be more receptive to the suggestion. Even those who originally turned down organized meals may appreciate the one-time offer. It is *how* you ask that makes the approach welcoming.

It is perfectly acceptable to leave food at someone's front or side door, letting them know you dropped something off, especially if the item(s) is perishable. A homemade freezer pack will ensure food safety. Whether it is breakfast items, a casserole, salad, soup, home-baked cookies, etc., the recipient can work what you dropped off into their menu that week or freeze it for later.

If you are unsure what to bring to someone in need, consider your favorite recipe that others have enjoyed. The entrée may be your go-to dinner on busy nights, something easy, effortless, and delicious. Consider the time of year. In spring and summer, light, bright, fresh foods are wonderful, such as grilled chicken, pork tenderloin, seafood, salads, and seasonal fruit and vegetables. In the fall and winter, warm, hearty foods are most comforting, such as pot roast, chicken pot pie, pasta, and soups. Perhaps you are known for a specific entrée, side dish, or dessert. Use that recipe and round out the rest of the meal with other items.

A meal delivery service can also be a good idea. Gift certificates can be purchased online and emailed to the recipient. The recipient can schedule meals or choose a restaurant close by.

For those who don't want to be disturbed, a Fill the Freezer opportunity (detailed below) may be a better option.

A meal team was offered during John's illness. As much as I appreciated it, it was not for me. I am much more comfortable giving than receiving. I have a hard time accepting help, but I had to learn to welcome outside assistance. I enjoy cooking, which was a distraction and escape, and I was fortunate to have someone stay with John while I ran to the store.

Reach out.

Fill the Freezer

Fill the Freezer is a wonderful option to support anyone in crisis. Freezer food can be collected from various groups (neighbors, coworkers, book club members, church groups, etc.) and delivered to someone in need. It is best to have an organizer oversee a Fill the Freezer opportunity to ascertain the needs, size of the family, and whether there are any dislikes, dietary restrictions, or allergies. The organizer should determine if the recipient has room in the freezer. If there is not ample freezer space, a volunteer can store the items until needed. Anyone providing a home-cooked meal for the freezer should label the items as described above. Do not feel the need to prepare homemade items for a Fill the Freezer outreach. Many delicious already-prepared frozen entrees and side dishes are available in the grocery store. Consider other frozen foods, such as fruits, vegetables, breakfast items, and ice cream or desserts. Those in crisis would appreciate any type of frozen items that can lighten their load. For those who may be susceptible to infections, packaged frozen food may be a better alternative than homemade items.

Again, be sure to find out if the recipient has freezer space. I know several families who were inundated with food. If you find this to be the case and you want to do something, a gift card to a local restaurant or grocery store is a supportive alternative that the recipient can use when needed.

Reach out.

Food Items

Anyone dealing with a troubling time would appreciate breakfast, lunch, dinner, snack, or dessert items. The recipient can either work what is dropped off into their menu in the next day or two or freeze it for later. A bagful of fresh fruit or snacks would be welcome any time. Be creative in what you bring, and keep in mind any dietary restrictions or allergies.

Even though I did not accept an organized meal team, friends left various food items on the front porch or by the side door. They texted me or left a voice message telling me they dropped something off. This was a pleasant surprise and so appreciated. I could either work the item(s) into my menu that week or freeze it for later. Homemade cookies were a real treat I kept in the freezer; I could grab one when I wanted.

A friend insisted on bringing me dinner from one of our favorite restaurants and asked what night would be good to drop off the meal. She did not ask if I wanted or needed a meal; she asked what *specific* day that week she could bring dinner. It is how she asked that made it easy for me to take her up on her offer. I picked a day, and she left dinner in the cooler on our front porch. She brought three or four main entrees, a large salad, dinner rolls, and home-baked cookies. What a special offering, and there was enough food for the next two nights. Her kindness definitely lightened my load, and we felt cared for.

Reach out.

Gift Cards

Any kind of gift card to a fast-food or sit-down restaurant, grocery store, drug store, chain store, meal delivery service, VISA-type, etc., is a thoughtful way to care for those dealing with a hardship when you want to do something but may be unsure how to proceed or time prevents you from helping in other ways The recipient can use the gift card to pick up a quick meal when there is no time to cook, when a break is needed following a tiring day, or to purchase needed items at the drugstore or a chain store. Any amount will be appreciated.

A gift card to a bookstore, salon, coffee shop, or local diner or restaurant is a caring gesture too, if you know the recipient may be able to use it. A gift card can be an unexpected surprise, a gracious gesture, and an act of kindness for anyone rooted in crisis.

A dear friend sent me a gift certificate to a local meal delivery service, which was a kindhearted present. I could schedule ready-to-eat meals twice a week, which gave me a little break from the kitchen. I also received a gift card to a local gelato store, and John thoroughly enjoyed this delicious treat. On several occasions, it was challenging to get him to eat anything, so I was happy to get something in him.

Reach out.

Flowers, Gifts, Treats, etc.

Flowers, gifts, and treats are wonderful ways to reach out. Your kindness may just be the encouraging highlight of someone's troubling day. Use your imagination, and if you know the family or friend well, a gift can be personalized to their interest. Anything you do will be uplifting and appreciated. Think outside the box and be creative. No one should ever feel alone or forgotten, whether it is the affected person, the immediate family, or the caregiver.

Numerous times, I passed by our front door and noticed flowers or gifts on the porch. Other items were sent through the mail from out-of-town friends. We were so touched to receive unexpected forms of outreach, and it warmed our hearts to know we were being thought of at a difficult time. Gestures such as these brightened our day and made our situation a bit more bearable.

A few gifts stood out when John was at home in hospice. In early October, a friend left a festive pumpkin on our porch. She later told me she was not sure it was appropriate but decided to deliver it anyway.

The pumpkin was a fun surprise, which I set in our living room, and John and I thought of her every time we passed by. Bottles of wine and snacks were left with notes indicating they were to be enjoyed at happy hour time. We also received homemade bread, a bouquet of happy-face cookies, a basket of breakfast items, homemade soup, home-baked cookies, a large poinsettia near Christmas, a bouquet of fresh flowers from a farmer's market, a basket addressed to me filled with thoughtful items that made me feel supported as a caregiver, and many more special, thoughtful items. These were heartwarming acts of kindness.

Reach out.

Offer to Run Errands, Complete Tasks, or Handle Routine Responsibilities

Many people dealing with a crisis may not have time during the day to handle everyday tasks or may not want to burden others by asking for help. Text or email that you are going out and ask if they need anything or offer to complete an errand. When you are specific in where you are going, it is a little easier for the recipient to ask for something to be picked up or for an errand to be completed. For example, let the recipient know that you are going to the grocery store on Wednesday morning, and ask what you can get for them, or say you are going to the pet store and you can pick up something their pet may need. If possible, give the recipient a few days' notice so there is ample time to put together a grocery list or consider what errands might be helpful.

A trying situation may entail daily trips for treatments such as physical therapy, chemotherapy, radiation, or visits to a hospital, a nursing home/health-care facility, etc. You need to reach out. Do not expect those knee-deep in a hardship to reach out to you as they may not have the time or energy to ask for help. Anything you can do to lessen someone's daily, weekly, or occasional responsibilities and demands is helpful, thoughtful, a genuine act of kindness, and much appreciated.

Reach out.

Child Care/Pet Care

Those in crisis may not have family members, friends, or neighbors nearby as helping hands for their children or pets. If you are comfortable, offer to babysit, walk the children to the bus stop, take them to after-school or weekend activities, or go out for a meal or ice cream, to a movie, to the library, to the park, etc. Perhaps letting the dog out during the day or taking it for a long walk, cleaning the cat's litter box, or feeding the pet could be helpful for those away from home for long periods of time during the day or who may be unable to leave the house even for a short time.

Reach out.

Offer to Accompany Someone to Doctor's Appointments and/or Treatments

If family members or friends are unable to accompany someone to a doctor's appointment, medical treatment, rehab therapy session, etc., offering to join them as another set of ears may be helpful, especially because it can be hard to remember everything or ask the right questions. Perhaps physical help is needed getting to and from an appointment, treatment, or therapy session. Having the company, another set of ears, and support from others means a lot.

Accompanying someone going through physical therapy or sitting with someone who is receiving chemotherapy or another medical treatment may just be the essential support needed. Even if they have local support, this may give a family member or caregiver a needed break from the circumstance, lightening their responsibilities.

Reach out.

Offer to Sit with Someone Who May Be Homebound or Ill

Whether in a hospital, health-care facility, or home setting, a caregiver may not have any spare time to make phone calls, schedule appointments, respond to emails, run errands, etc. Offer to sit with the affected person so the caregiver can have a break from the situation or get things done. It is important to be on time as the caregiver is counting on the commitment you made.

Reach out.

Offer to Accompany Someone to a Funeral Home, Cemetery, or House of Worship

The death of someone special is something for which no one is ever truly prepared. Perhaps the death was expected following a tragic accident or chronic illness, but maybe it was a sudden, unforeseen occurrence. If the survivor does not have local support, offer to accompany them to begin the funeral arrangements. Your suggestion may or may not be welcome, but you don't know unless you ask. Having the company of another may provide essential support, and an extra set of ears may be helpful when making final plans.

Once someone enters hospice, death is most likely imminent, and as difficult as it is to think about, it is beneficial to get any inevitable arrangements started. This can be a very sensitive area. Some people may be in denial, unable to accept the unfortunate outcome or feel a visit to a funeral home or cemetery prior to death is unwarranted at the time. Preplanning a funeral, making cemetery preparations, drafting a memorial service, and discussing end-of-life arrangements can be uncomfortable and unpleasant. This is an extremely emotional time, and once someone has passed away, it is even harder to think clearly when making final decisions. If you are a family member or close friend or know the caregiver does not have a lot of support, offer to accompany them when visiting a potential funeral home, cemetery, or house of worship to begin the process. Helping in this area can be emotionally supportive, and, again, another set of ears is always valuable, as well as having a sound shoulder to lean on at an emotional time.

                Reach out.

Coworkers, Neighbors, Acquaintances

If someone in your circle is experiencing a trying time, touch base to uncover what you can do to lessen the hardship. Those affected may not have local support to lend assistance or may find it hard to ask for help. Perhaps they are doing okay; consider what you can do to brighten an unsettling day. Draw on previous examples. Think outside the box.

                Reach out.

People in Crisis Living in an Apartment or Condominium

If you want to deliver something to someone living in an apartment or condominium, determine the easiest way to drop it off. It may be fine leaving something at the front door, or perhaps there is a neighbor who can accept it if they're not physically there to receive it. You might also ask when someone might be home to accept the item.

    If it's not convenient to deliver something due to the location of the building or if it is a gated community, a gift card is a wonderful alternative. A gift card can simply be put in a note or greeting card and wrapped in several sheets of blank paper or bubble wrap to ensure the security of the gift card before placing it in an envelope to mail.

                Reach out.

Suggestions to Lend Support for Those Living Out of Town

Be mindful that no one truly knows what others may be going through and the challenges or obstacles they may be up against, especially if those affected are not local. Whatever you can do to lessen someone's troubles speaks volumes. Some suggestions for out-of-town support include:

Cards. Sending a note of concern can brighten up a down day when those struggling may feel alone, stressed, overwhelmed, or isolated. *Thinking of you at this difficult time* is appropriate wording, showing empathy and thoughtful regard to any kind of troubling issue.

Food. There are many websites showcasing fruit or snack baskets, cheese trays, entrée items, desserts, etc. These sites safely package food items that can be delivered to a home or business address. Be sure a thinking-of-you note accompanies the item so the recipient knows who sent the gift.

Gift Cards. Any type of gift card can alleviate the stress of those in crisis. If you purchase a gift card and intend to send it through the mail, be sure to wrap it in several sheets of blank paper or bubble wrap to ensure security before placing it in an envelope to mail with a thinking-of-you note.

Flowers/Plants. A seasonal plant, bouquet of fresh flowers, or greenhouse plant can be a beacon of light during a dark time. There are many easily accessible websites for floral deliveries, or your local florist can assist in this process. A thinking-of-you note is all it needs.

Reach out.

Hospital, Rehabilitation/Treatment Facility, and Home Visits

When someone is in the hospital for tests, treatments, surgery, or rehabilitation or at home recovering from a health issue, find out if visits are welcome. Those hurting may or may not want or be able to have visitors. Regardless of your relationship with the person or family, rest and privacy should be at the forefront. You do not want to tire someone out who truly needs rest. If popping in is welcome, make a point to stop by. The visit should be brief. Dropping by speaks volumes, and you only need to acknowledge that the person has been in your thoughts and prayers. Do not go empty-handed. If you have time to pick something up, anything would be appreciated such as flowers, a plant, a balloon, magazines, etc. There are no magic words you can say, especially if the situation is difficult; your visit shows you care, which is important and meaningful to the patient and/or family.

Many people feel uneasy and apprehensive about visiting someone in the hospital, rehab center, treatment facility, or home setting, especially when the prognosis or predicament is grim. Others may turn away from a disturbing circumstance or a terminally ill person, perhaps feeling edgy, find it difficult to process the troublesome issue, or maybe pondering their own mortality. Situations can hit a little too close to home, but do not shy away from someone's current ordeal. Remember it is not about you and how unsettled you may feel; it is about the person and family dealing with a troubling period. Those suffering will most likely welcome a friendly face and short visit. *I've been thinking of you* is all that needs to be conveyed. Your presence speaks louder than words.

A visit should be a pleasant encounter, showing empathy and support; whatever form of backing you can provide is meaningful. I have heard others remark how troubling it is to hear complaints from visitors while they are enduring a tragedy, in recovery, terminally ill, or undergoing another difficult adversity. The focus of any visit should be on those dealing with a real hardship, not you or anyone else. It is important not to share any similar situation you may have had or knew someone who did. Even though you may have knowledge of a comparable occurrence, everyone is individual, and everyone's circumstance is different. No one wants to hear what you or someone you knew had gone through unless you are specifically asked to share your insights or experiences.

If someone is in the hospital or other facility for several days or longer, snacks (nutrition bars, individual packages of crackers, snack mix, nuts, apples or other fruit, mints, gum, small bottles of water, magazines, newspapers, puzzle books, etc.) are a thoughtful gesture for family members or friends to nibble on while sitting with the patient day in and day out or for visitors who stop by.

If hospital, rehabilitation, or home visits are shunned, honor the patient's, families', or doctors' wishes for rest and privacy. As much as you may want to see and support the patient, be respectful of anyone who truly needs quiet time to heal and recover, unconditional privacy, or who may be terminally ill. There are many ways you can lend support when visits are discouraged. A note of concern, flowers, or gift item can be left on the recipient's front porch if you know someone will be returning home during the day or brought to the hospital or other facility and left with the receptionist or at the nurses' station. Be sure to include a personal note so the recipient knows who the gesture is from. *Thinking of you* is all that needs to be conveyed. A simple expression of concern sent through the mail is always appropriate and appreciated if you prefer to reach out in this way.

Reach out.

Children Encountering a Troubling Period

Anyone with a child going through a tumultuous period, whether a weighty mental or physical issue, medical tests, or surgery unquestionably needs assistance and support. I have previously outlined many suggestions to lend backing to those in crisis, yet there are additional ways to reach out when a child is experiencing a troubling ordeal:

- **Deliver toys, books, or fun surprises** to raise the spirits of the child affected or their sibling(s), especially if the parents

are spending a lot of time at the hospital and/or away from home.
- **Drop off a meal or frozen entrée item(s).**
- **Food.** Deliver family-friendly snacks for kids' lunches or for parents who may be at the hospital or other facility.
- **Child care.** If there are siblings, you can babysit, walk them to the bus stop, pick them up, take them to activities, or take them somewhere fun.
- **Laundry.** Ask the family to leave their laundry outside their door in the morning to be washed, dried, folded, and returned later in the day.
- **Paper products.** Drop off regularly used paper and household products such as foil, plastic wrap, garbage bags, sandwich bags, tissues, toilet paper, paper towels, paper plates, paper cups, and plasticware.
- **Drop off diapers and wipes** if you know the size of the baby or toddler.
- **Cash.** Drop off cash for the parents, with a note indicating the intention for the money (fast-food restaurant, hospital cafeteria, parking lot fees, valet services, gas); any amount will be appreciated.
- **Give a gift card** to a restaurant, grocery store, drug store, chain store, etc.
- **Yard work.** Can you mow the grass, water plants, rake leaves, or shovel snow?
- **Housekeeping.** Offer to do routine chores or chip in with a group for a cleaning service.

Reach out.

Young Families Enduring a Troubling Time

Perhaps you know a young family in the thick of a health crisis, job loss, financial strain, or other adversity; support is crucial. The parents may be attempting to keep their lives as normal as possible. This can be confusing for the whole family. If the family is open to outside assistance, there are many ways to reach out to lighten their load; use the above list as guidance.

If a family asks for privacy, the request should be honored. You can reach out by discreetly dropping off an item from the above suggested list. A note of concern is always appropriate and appreciated. A family in crisis should never feel alone or forgotten. Think outside the box and consider what would be helpful if you were in a comparable situation.

Reach out.

Fundraisers

A crisis can put a financial strain on anyone regardless of what the circumstance or predicament may be. The stress of paying bills, medical invoices, credit card statements, attorney fees, car loans, mortgages, and other outstanding accounts can add another hazy layer to a hardship. If this is the case, a fundraiser may be a welcome opportunity. Ask the affected person or family if a fundraiser would be beneficial. A community-wide drive or social media-based site may help raise funds for a specific cause. If the suggestion of a fundraiser is welcome, an organizer should oversee the process with help from volunteers.

Reach out.

Common Struggles and Troublesome Times

There are no guarantees in life. Adversities happen.

Crumbling Relationships, Separation, Divorce

Sensitivity should be center stage for those enduring a crumbling relationship, separation, or divorce. This can be an emotionally devastating period despite the circumstances; support is central. There may be nothing you can do to remedy the situation or even attempt to help to resolve the predicament, but reaching out is essential. Show up and respond in a sincere way. Touch base often as the hurting person may be experiencing a roller-coaster of emotions and struggling to move in a more positive direction. Be mindful that the rocky time and rippling effects may linger for many months, a year, or longer. Children may be in the middle of the trying period, which may add additional concerns to an already distressing stretch.

Whatever you can do to lend an understanding ear to someone's worries is thoughtful and may provide much-needed emotional support. Depending on the situation, someone may need temporary housing, help looking for a place to live, aid in moving, or assistance in finding other employment. No one should ever feel alone or forgotten during any tumultuous period.

Small gestures, as listed above, may be the highlight of someone's day when his or her world has turned upside down, and life's path may now be filled with many onerous hurdles and uncertainties.

What support can you offer?

Reach out.

Job Loss

Anyone receiving upsetting news of a work layoff or job loss may experience a wide range of perplexing emotions. The announcement may have been expected, but perhaps it came out of the blue. The unstable feelings and financial strains can be difficult for anyone to process. Whatever you can do to encourage, boost, and support those enduring a foreboding time is critical. There may be nothing you can do to remedy the situation, but lending a neutral ear to the affected person's worries and conflicts can be significant. You may have a job connection to pass on or know of someone looking for new hires. Again, no one should feel alone or abandoned when experiencing a trying time; support from others is vital. Put yourself in someone else's shoes. What would help you if you were in an identical situation?

Reach out.

Financial Strains

Financial hardship can happen at any time. Perhaps it was anticipated, but possibly it occurred without any warning. At times, meeting basic needs can become a challenge for many people and families. The adversity may be from a layoff or job loss, a crumbling relationship, child support or alimony, poor budgeting, careless spending, credit card bills, volatile financial markets, student loans, car obligations, mortgage payments, mounting debts, etc. Financial strains can result in tremendous stress on a person's health as well as everyday life and relationships. There may be nothing you can do to help someone recover or overcome financial struggles and challenges, but reaching out and offering an unbiased ear and words of encouragement may be the backing needed for someone to move in a more favorable direction. Can you be there for someone facing financial misfortunes by being a nonsubjective listener and/or lending emotional sustenance to another's worries?

Reach out.

First-Time Parents or Family Additions

As thrilled as first-time parents are for their newborn, support is key as they face a whole new world of learning to care for their infant, not to mention the many months of sleepless nights. Yes, local family members may be available to offer immediate assistance, but additional help may be very comforting to new parents. Refer to the suggestions above on ways to offer help. Anything you can do to lighten a family's daily responsibilities is a kind gesture.

Parents are often spread thin with added responsibilities when another child comes into the family unit—a newly blended family, temporary foster care, or adoption. Think outside the box and offer assistance that you feel may be beneficial.

Reach out.

Minor Struggles

This book emphasizes reaching out to those dealing with major obstacles. However, connecting with those going through minor problems is just as paramount. Support should be offered to those dealing with a cold, the flu, dental surgery, outpatient or inpatient surgery, a sprained ankle, a new baby, a car in the repair shop, a relative or friend on deployment, etc. Those who live alone or don't have family or friends nearby may need extra help. Can you check in offering needed assistance?

Several winters ago, I had a terrible cold and was advised to stay home, get rest, and avoid contact with others for a week. When a friend learned of my sickness, she left a bag at my front door. Inside were two containers of soup, a smoothie, tea bags, throat lozenges, and several magazines. Her thoughtfulness brightened my day, and I thoroughly enjoyed the freshly made soups rather than the canned chicken noodle soup in my pantry. Be creative. Do what you can to make a difficulty, big or small, a little bit easier.

Reach out.

Other Difficult Situations

When overwhelmed, stressed, burned out, or lost in life, whether it is a result of a complicated relationship, work issues, challenges of daily living, depression, anxiety, mental or physical abuse, struggling with an eating disorder, surprised with an unexpected intervention, thoughts of or attempted suicide, overindulgence of alcohol, substance abuse or overdose, abortion, or jail or prison, support is vital. A call, note, meal, or gift can brighten the affected person's day.

Depending on the circumstance, make a point to stop by. It may be uncomfortable to see someone dealing with an unfortunate situation, but keep in mind it's not about you and how awkward you may feel; it's about someone battling a real problem. The visit does not need to be long, and your presence speaks volumes. You only need to convey that you are thinking of him or her during a difficult period.

If someone is in a treatment-type setting and the facility is open to patients receiving outside items, delivering a best-seller book, current magazine, or other gift item is a thoughtful gesture. Suggestions for a gift basket are listed below if you are unsure what kind of items you may want to include. Regardless of what the circumstance may have been, if someone is struggling for a few months or possibly years, frequently touching base gives essential support to those who may feel alone.

Reach out.

Rehabilitation Facilities

Be mindful of anyone combating an addiction regardless of what the dependency may be. If you are close to the person and visitors are welcome, pay a visit if you are able. It may be thorny visiting someone in their setting, but it is not about you and how uneasy you may feel; it is about someone going through an unfortunate, troubling period. Do not shy away, dodge, or disappear from anyone dealing with an addiction or emotional problem seeking to find his or her way in the world. Those at the height of any kind of encumbrance need support. There are no magic words to say when you meet up; your presence shows you care, and that is what is important. Your visit does not need to be long, and acknowledging to the affected person that he or she has been on your mind is all that needs to be conveyed. Stopping by will be a welcome distraction during a lonely, gray stretch.

If you can visit someone in a treatment or rehab facility and you have time to pick something up, anything you bring is a thoughtful, caring gesture. Check with the facility to determine if outside items are allowed.

If someone is unable to have visitors or receive outside items, send a note through the mail; showing support can brighten a dreary, somber day. Understandably, it can be difficult to know what to write in a note when someone is in a treatment facility. Even if a card has a printed verse, write a personal message expressing you are thinking of them. Send several notes or cards if the commitment continues for several months or longer. If you are close to the affected family, show them emotional support as their lives are embroiled in the situation just as much as the one who is receiving treatment.

Reach out.

Assisted Living, Nursing Home, Health-Care Facility, or the Homebound

Sending thinking of you, birthday, and seasonal cards is uplifting, meaningful, appropriate, and welcome. The resident may be lonely, and reaching out in this way is a genuine act of kindness.

If you are able, try to stop by someone's current location. Your visit may just be the highlight of his or her day or week, and do not go empty-handed if possible. A few suggested items are a seasonal decoration or easy-to-care-for house plant, fresh flowers, current magazines or books, snacks, etc. Should you choose to put together a gift bag or basket, the contents can be personalized to the person's interests, situation, or health issues. Suggestions are highlighted below. If someone is not up to a visit, the gift bag can be left at the receptionist's desk or at the recipient's front door with a note that you are thinking of him or her.

Reach out.

Pregnancy Complications/Miscarriage

I have frequently heard others remark they are at a loss for words when a friend, coworker, neighbor, acquaintance, or family member experiences a pregnancy complication or miscarriage. Keep in mind it is not about how ill at ease you may feel in not knowing what to say; it is about the person, couple, and/or family who are going through a heartbreaking period. Sensitivity should be the prominent focus when speaking with the affected parent(s) or the immediate family. Realize that there may be nothing you can say or do to make things better, but letting those hurting know they are thought of at a difficult time means a lot. Sending a note of concern is always proper and appreciated.

If a miscarriage occurred, do not lose sight of the fact that a loss is a loss regardless of when it happened in the pregnancy. When and if you run into the couple, acknowledge the tragedy, and state you are thinking of them. A warm hug or gentle touch on the arm or shoulder shows compassion and empathy. Do not shy away from responding to the heartbreaking period; avoiding the subject when you see or talk to the couple can be hurtful and perhaps leave them wondering why you did not mention their misfortune. If you want to do something and are unsure how to proceed, a thinking-of-you card, flowers, or house plant are sincere ways to acknowledge the loss.

Reach out.

Tragic/Horrific Ordeals

A tragic/horrific ordeal or situation can occur at any moment and forever change the lives of those involved and anyone connected with the affected individual(s), family, friends, group, and possibly outsiders. Perhaps the traumatic incident was somewhat expected, but maybe it was totally unforeseen, without any early, obvious, threatening warning signs. The occurrence may have been misguided, unfamiliar, foreign, vicious, deviant, twisted, or warped, leaving those touched brokenhearted, outraged, full of hate, permanently scarred, emotionally and physically detached from others and life, and incredibly alone, devasted, and haunted.

Disturbing situations can justifiably be awkward and uncomfortable, but that should not prevent anyone from responding to a tragedy. Acknowledge the troubling ordeal, showing heartfelt compassion and support to those hurting and/or suffering. How can outsiders respond to unbearable, horrendous events? Can you reach out to those tormented with heartache and dire straits through acts of kindness or provide other caring gestures? If you run into those affected, a firm, sympathetic hug stating *you've been in my thoughts and prayers* is all that needs to be conveyed. No one can remedy a broken heart, alter what happened, or reverse what occurred, yet responding to another's distressing ordeal can radiate a slight glimpse of light when times may be very dark and painful.

Reach out.

Hospice

When someone has entered a hospice program, death is most likely near and imminent. This can be an extremely unfortunate, unsettling, and sorrowful time no matter what the circumstance may be. Heavy emotions, anxiety, stress, sadness, and the uncertainties of what may lie ahead can be bewildering and heartbreaking. The person and/or the family may be experiencing a short or long questionable, agonizing period. Sending an expression of kindness is heartwarming and thoughtful and may be the essential support needed for those in crisis to just get through the day and the coming days.

If visits are permitted, stop by at a time that is convenient for the family. There is no question that it may be unsettling to connect with someone who is in hospice. Again, it is not about you and how apprehensive you may feel seeing someone in their current situation or setting; it is about the suffering person and his or her family and the somber time they are in. If you have time to pick something up, do not go emptyhanded. Your visit does not need to be long and the only thing that needs to be expressed is that you are thinking about him or her and wanted to stop by. If you are a family member, close friend, long-time co-worker, neighbor, fellow church member, etc., shying away from visiting anyone terminally ill is inexcusable. Step outside of uncomfortable situations. Show up. Be present. Offer support.

Reach out.

Home Emergencies

Anyone experiencing a casualty due to a water main break, storm damage, loss of electrical power, fire, or other unexpected major home disaster may be in desperate need of assistance. What can you do to help someone when a sudden emergency occurs? Can you drop off cleaning products suitable for the particular adversity (a bucket, cloth rags, sponges, brushes, a mop, soap, paper towels, etc.)? Can you deliver a meal? Can you drop off a case of bottled water? Can you donate items to help others get back on their feet (canned food, kitchen necessities, everyday household items, bath towels, trash bags, clothing, personal products, etc.)? Can you provide temporary shelter or housing? A neighborhood group, coworkers, friends, church family, or a community association can pull together to assist those who have suffered a devastating ordeal. Gift cards to big-box stores, grocery stores, drug stores, or restaurants are always welcome to fill in the gaps of everyday essentials.

Reach out.

Natural Disasters

When a natural disaster occurs (flood, tornado, hurricane, tsunami, earthquake, fire, winter ice/snowstorm, etc.), aren't we all called to reach out and respond to our fellow humans? Assistance from families, friends, coworkers, neighbors, churches, or community groups can be a vital lifeline. What would help you if you were in a similar situation? Can you help find temporary housing? Although gift cards to chain stores, grocery stores, and restaurants are always appreciated, a business may not be open depending on the disaster that occurred.

Reach out.

Additional Thoughts

*It is important to understand that everyone deals
with a crisis and the aftermath differently.
No one truly knows what someone has faced or may
have gone through.
Everyone has a story, a personal journey.*

Ask

*A*sk is a common, everyday word I find somewhat jarring. It can put the recipient in an awkward position of having to respond, which may feel uncomfortable and troublesome despite the nature of the hardship. However, occasionally, there are instances when the needs of those struggling can be vague and doubtful, and you may need to question what might be helpful if you are truly at a loss for how to lend assistance. Those suffering may find it hard to ask for help; they may not want to burden others with their circumstances or problems, may attempt to handle challenges on their own, may not know what assistance will be beneficial, or perhaps truly want and/or need privacy. Anyone experiencing a trying situation may not have the time or energy to reach out for support, but making them aware that you are available to lend a helping hand is important. You may not be able to provide immediate assistance, but perchance you know someone who can, or you can help uncover outside resources.

It is *how* you ask that may be most welcoming for those in crisis. The recipient may feel more comfortable accepting assistance when you are specific in what you are offering. If your offer is accepted, it is imperative to be on time. I have heard several people remark that they have had to reschedule appointments or necessary errands when the person lending assistance was late or never showed up, leaving them frustrated and, therefore, scrambling to make other arrangements.

Reach out.

Medical Equipment or Essential Items

If you have or know of someone who has medical equipment or other essential items not being used, offer these goods to those in need. Transport chairs, wheelchairs, walkers, canes, bedside commodes, shower seats, bed trays, TV-tray stands, wheelchair ramps, a crib, baby gates, a highchair, etc., may not be needed at the present time, but they could be crucial down the road. Perhaps a family could use a large cooler to set on their front porch for meals being dropped off on a regular basis.

Several friends offered various medical supplies during John's health issues, which I quickly realized might be useful. I borrowed a transport chair and a shower seat, which became necessary pieces of equipment for the challenges we were encountering. When a friend's husband had hip surgery several years ago, I offered a TV-tray stand I was not using, and they were very appreciative to borrow it.

Reach out.

Listen

Those in crisis often need the compassionate ears of others as they deal with troubling concerns and worries. Sharing their raw emotions, daily struggles, painful challenges, troubling fears, anxieties, or venting may be paramount for them. Their feelings may be compounding or bottled up, or they may be stuck in emotional turmoil, unable to see any hint of light at the end of a long, wearisome, dark tunnel. Be prepared to hear disturbing information or graphic details should someone need to share the grim particulars. Do not feel the need to respond or the urgency to provide a solution or an answer to their troubles. Most often, there is nothing anyone can say or do to change a tumultuous time, but lending a nonjudgmental ear could be what's needed the most. It is so simple. Just listen.

Listening to a family's or caregiver's concerns may shed light on their needs that they may or may not even be aware of. For example, when I mentioned that John was unsteady on his feet, a friend immediately offered her mother's transport chair, which I quickly accepted. We really needed this step-down wheelchair, and we put many miles on it. I was so appreciative. Aware of our challenges, another friend offered a shower seat, which I instantly realized we could use. After sharing with a friend that the physical therapist advised me to have a wheelchair ramp at the house when John was released from rehab, she and her husband sprang into action. I came home a few days later and was surprised to see they built and installed a wheelchair ramp on our back deck. Listen. Pay attention. Lend a helpful, sympathetic ear, and respond if you are able.

Reach out.

Caregivers

Regardless of the nature of the hardship, a caregiver, whether it is a spouse, parent, child, or paid employee, shoulders a huge weight, and they are often overlooked and forgotten. Caregiving may be a short-term stretch or continue for many years. Providing care is an all-consuming role from the minute a caregiver's feet touch the floor each morning until the sun sets or later. Caregivers may be responsible for bathing, dressing, preparing meals, helping at mealtimes, maintaining mental and physical health, keeping up with occupational and physical therapy, shuttling to and from doctor's appointments, housekeeping, etc.—as well as anything unexpected that may occur any time during the day or in the middle of the night.

There is nothing harder than caring for someone with a handicap, mentally or physically, someone experiencing a serious injury or illness, unforeseen or not, or the elderly. The aid and attention provided is immeasurable, and caregivers can be easily become overwhelmed and fall into deep depression, vulnerability, and loss of self. Caregivers should be put on a pedestal for their sacrifices. They do it out of love, yet they can be underappreciated. Caregivers need a break to regroup, recharge, and refresh their emotional beings so they can return to their responsibilities in a renewed light.

A caregiver's days can be long and emotionally and physically draining. Whatever you can do to cheer up, lighten their workload, or provide needed support is significant. Cards, meals, gifts, or time away from the situation are always appreciated and may give the caregiver the courage, energy, and strength to get through each day.

Reach out.

Remember Other Family Members

Family members also carry a hefty weight of their loved one's troubles or illness. Feelings of concern, worry, anxiety, stress, and/or uncertainty about the precarious road ahead may be all-consuming for the immediate family and others affected.

Yes, I was dealing with my husband's terminal illness, but my children were also coping with their dad's fatal diagnosis and all the added heartbreaking emotions—sadness, fear, helplessness, etc. Any type of support you can provide other family members may help their troubling ordeal seem a little bit more bearable. Support to the immediate family members is uplifting and a thoughtful, kind outreach.

Reach out.

Reach Out—Be Creative

It is hard to keep any sense of normalcy for anyone navigating a crisis. Offer to do *specific* things that have been mentioned earlier or think outside the box. If a holiday is approaching, purchase Easter or Halloween candy, address seasonal cards, shop for gifts, decorate for the holidays, etc. If needs are not readily apparent, you may need to ask precisely what you can do to ease or lessen any worries or burdens.

Knowing I was going through a devastating time, I received an email from a church friend. She offered to come to our home to set up and decorate our Christmas tree. I was surprised by her suggestion as this idea never would have occurred to me. Although I did not take her up on it, I appreciated her reaching out to me. What can you do to lighten the load of someone struggling?

Reach out.

More Ways to Reach Out

Many suggestions to lend support to those in crisis have been previously presented; however, if you are still unsure how to help someone in the thick of a distressing time or are looking for additional ways to lend assistance, these suggestions may be considered:

Physical Assistance. Perhaps physical help is needed in getting someone safely out of the house to a doctor's appointment, treatment session, or other scheduled meeting as well as back home.

Gas. Can you fill up their car or drop off a gift card for a nearby service station?

Routine vehicle maintenance. Perhaps assistance is needed in getting someone's vehicle serviced. Whether it is a standard oil change, yearly inspection, or car troubles, those dealing with a hardship may not have the time to complete the task, and offering to accomplish this undertaking may be helpful.

Reach out.

Gift Bags/Gift Baskets

If you want to do something special, a gift bag or basket is a thoughtful gesture and is easy to put together and can be left at the recipient's front door, delivered to the person in the hospital, left at the nurses' station, or other known location. This idea is purely a suggestion depending on your relationship with the affected person, cost, and available time you have to put it together. A thinking-of-you card is all that needs to be included.

Putting together a gift bag or basket is simple, and it can be as small or as large as you choose. The contents can be personalized to their interests, health issues, or circumstances. (If someone is not up to reading, you would not want to include a book or other printed material. If the person is on a restricted diet, you would not want to include certain food items, etc.). Use your judgment and be creative, especially if you know the individual well. Some suggestions are:

- Notepad/journal
- Pens/pencils/colored pencils/crayons/washable markers
- Coloring books
- Magazines
- Crossword/word search/Suduko puzzle book
- Jigsaw puzzle
- Game for one or two players
- Playing cards
- Mints/gum
- Snacks
- Socks/slippers
- Drink tumbler/insulated tumbler
- Toiletry items (lotion, toothpaste, toothbrush, deodorant, comb, hairbrush, mirror, tissues)
- Toiletry bag (to hold toiletry items)
- Wipes/sanitizer
- Washable throw

- Stuffed animals
- Toys (car, Legos, bubbles, doll, etc.)

Reach out.

Chemotherapy or Other Medical Treatments

Anyone going through chemotherapy or other medical care may face many months or possibly years of treatment and/or unexpected setbacks or hospital stays. This can be a long, difficult, and uncertain time for the person.

If you want to do a little something more than a note of concern, a washable tote bag, found at most craft stores or big-box stores, filled with useful items can be left at the person's front door prior to the start or at the beginning of the regimen. Suggested items to include in the bag are listed above, but additional ideas are

- Small bottles of ginger ale
- Tea bags
- Saltine crackers
- Small blanket

I have given tote bags filled with useful items to several people starting chemotherapy, and they were appreciative of the bag and the goodies inside. One gal said she almost felt excited to start chemotherapy, not that she was truly thrilled. She said it felt like it was the first day of the school year with a brand-new backpack.

Reach out.

When the Waves of Emotions Continue

Anything you can do to lessen someone's worries, responsibilities, and demands is helpful, thoughtful, a genuine act of kindness, and much appreciated by those enduring challenging times.

Just Because

When something is given unexpectedly, it can be uplifting and undeniably brightens an overcast day. If you have additional servings from a meal or extra cookies you just baked, drop off the item(s) in a disposable container with a note that you were thinking of the recipient. Maybe you saw a cute holiday decoration while shopping, current magazines caught your eye as you were checking out at the grocery store, or perhaps picking up a seasonal plant will undoubtedly cheer someone up—just because. If you do not want to disturb those hurting, leave what you brought at the recipient's front door or with the facility's receptionist and call or text the person to whom you left something.

A gift basket, large or small, will certainly raise anyone's spirits. A themed basket is another thoughtful idea, especially if you know the person well. Here are some ideas for *just because* baskets tailored to the person:

- *Sunshine* basket—anything yellow. A journal, napkins, socks, candle, washable throw, etc.

- *Reader's* basket—books, magazines, puzzles, journal, pen, book light, reading glasses, bookstore gift card, washable throw, etc.
- *Cook's* basket—notepad, cooking magazines, cookbook, bookmark, blank recipe cards, cooking utensils, measuring spoons, measuring cups, spices, hot pads, dish towel, apron, etc.
- *Gardener's* basket—gardening magazines or books, a journal, pen, notepad, garden gloves, kneepad, seed packets, hand shovel, green or blooming plant, fresh herbs, gift card to a local nursery, etc.
- *Game* basket—playing cards, crossword puzzle, sudoku, pens/pencils, notepad, jigsaw puzzle, board games, etc.
- *Movie* basket—popcorn, snacks, candy, beverages, drink tumbler, colorful napkins, washable throw, etc.
- *Coffee Lover* basket—variety of coffees, flavored creamers or syrups, coffee mug, travel mug, biscotti, a gift card to a chain or local coffee shop, etc.
- *Breakfast* basket—donuts, fresh fruit, croissants, muffins, coffee cake, bagels, cream cheese, jelly, granola, cereal, coffee, tea, bottled juice(s), napkins, etc.
- *Snack* basket—popcorn, chips, crackers, candy, bottles or canned beverages, colorful napkins, etc.
- *Love* basket—anything red, chocolate or candy bars; notepad, pen, candles, a gift card for a pedicure, manicure, massage, or bookstore, washable throw, etc.
- *New Parent* basket—family magazines, parenting books, bottled water, flavored decaf coffee, snacks, fresh fruit, burp cloths, diapers, wipes, children's books, stuffed animals, gift cards, etc.
- *Pet* basket—pet toy, treats, brush, leash, water or food bowl, disposable plastic bags, collar, pet store gift card, etc.
- *Prayer* basket—devotional or inspirational book, bookmark,

notepad, journal, pen, candle, washable throw; etc.
- *Monday through Sunday* basket—small gifts with days-of-the-week labels to unwrap as a fun surprise that day.

The ideas for a themed basket are endless. Use your imagination and think outside the box.

Reach out.

Sensitive Dates and Holidays

Be mindful that certain dates and holidays may be a sensitive time. The hustle and bustle of a holiday is a happy and joyful occasion, but not for those deeply entangled in a distressing period. Traditions may have changed or, at the very least, may never be the same. Reach out, acknowledging how difficult you can only imagine this time may be.

Reach out.

Show Up. Be There. Be Present

I cannot stress enough the importance of showing up, being there, and being present for anyone in crisis; support is crucial. We can all be easily distracted by everyday life happenings, and if you say you are going to be there for someone who is dealing with a trying circumstance, do not lose touch or disappear.

Do not feel slighted if you have reached out to extend support and your offer is turned down or goes unanswered. Often, those affected may pull back and find it difficult to be open to outside communications or accept backing of any kind. Continue to reach out on a regular basis. Those struggling may just need a shoulder to lean on, a compassionate ear to listen, or simply something dropped off, such as a loaf of bread, a gallon of milk, or a bag of pet food. Can you be that kind of support system? Can you provide a safety net during someone's challenges?

Whether it was a text, phone call, or short visit from family members or friends, I could not have gotten through the heartbreaking six months John was ill without their kindness, love, and support. I had more emotional baggage on my full, overflowing plate than I ever imagined while juggling daily responsibilities and demands, and knowing I could unload my feelings on those willing to listen or ask for assistance helped me get through an unbearable time. Knowing others were there for my family and me held us up on many challenging days.

Reach out.

Just Do

The needs of those in crisis are not always readily apparent or obvious. Depending on your relationship with those struggling, you may need to *just do*. The affected person or family may be so overwhelmed with what is on their unwieldly plate that they may not know what they need or may not have the time or emotional fuel to ask for assistance. Do not sit back and wait to be asked to do something. *Just do*. There is no question that reaching out and responding unexpectedly is extremely thoughtful and meaningful. If you think something would be beneficial and is the right thing to do, it probably is. *Just do*.

Reach out.

Do the Unexpected

Those enduring a hardship may be stressed and/or exhausted following a long, taxing day, and receiving unexpected kind gestures, such as returning home to find that the grass has been cut or the trash can or recycling bin was brought back up to the house, can turn an overwhelming, demanding day around. Acts of kindness always brighten up difficult days. There are countless ways to lend support.

Additional helpful ways to support those in crisis include bringing the newspaper or mail to the front door, washing, drying, and folding a load or two of laundry, pulling weeds that may be taking over a flower bed, watering outdoor plants, putting out mulch to freshen up an outdoor garden area, raking leaves in the fall, shoveling snow on a walkway or clearing two tire tracks in the driveway so the recipient can leave the house if necessary.

As I mentioned earlier, John and I were surprised when a couple we hardly knew paid for our dinner one night following one of his radiation treatments. Their unexpected kindness was touching.

Another family we did not know well sent us a VISA gift card that we used to pick up a quick dinner a couple of times following a long, tiring day. I will never forget these special people and their sincere act of kindness.

Reach out.

Acknowledgment

If you are aware of someone's troubling time, regardless of what the circumstance may be, avoiding the predicament can be hurtful and, frankly, inexcusable. Too many times, outsiders shy away from addressing another's problems for many reasons. Perhaps they are hesitant to speak up, not knowing what to say to someone impacted by a crisis. The plight may be totally foreign, or situations may possibly hit a little too close to home, which is understandable. Be mindful that it is not about you and how hesitant you may feel in not knowing what to say or do; it is about those going through a really difficult time. There is no question that challenging ordeals are precarious, as well as outsiders who genuinely want to help. Uneasiness should not stand between you and those dealing with a tumultuous period.

Acknowledging another's tragic period is crucial. Avoiding the situation can seem puzzling to those in crisis. Why are others acting like it is just another day when they are aware of our stormy ordeal? I am sure my friends, neighbors, coworkers, and church family have heard of my troubles, yet no one has called, sent a note, or acknowledged our struggles when they see me. Do outsiders not realize they will be on the receiving end of a distressing time at some point in their lives?

Approach those suffering by simply stating, "I heard your family is dealing with some difficult issues, and I just want you to know that I'm thinking of you." If you can lend a helping hand, you can add, "I'm happy to help out in any way, whether it's picking up needed items at the grocery store or drugstore or dropping off a meal." Offering hands-on assistance is helpful, yet often a sympathetic, nonjudgmental ear may be what is needed. Step outside of yourself and set aside any feelings of uneasiness to confront a distressing situation directly with words of empathy, compassion, and support, as well as acts of kindness.

Reach out.

Prayers

Many people need and rely on prayer for spiritual support, comfort, and peace and/or to hold on to hope as they encounter and attempt to deal with their crisis. Prayers may provide much-needed encouragement, positivity, and holy connections during dark, rocky times. A prayer chain or prayer group can be organized to reach out to a large assembly to enhance divine bonds and backing to those experiencing challenges. Sending a note to someone needing prayers, stating you are keeping them in your thoughts and praying for them, is meaningful too and can be uplifting, giving added strength to those struggling and hurting. Whatever you can do to offer prayerful support may be paramount for those needing spiritual and religious comfort.

Reach out.

Keep In Mind

A crisis is about those dealing with a troubling time or loss. Step outside of yourself; it's not about you.

Step Outside of Yourself; It's Not About You

I have heard many people voice their frustration when others fail to listen, provide a sympathetic, reassuring ear, or lend practical action-based support. Too often, outsiders unintentionally want to offer a Band-Aid solution or definitive answer to someone's troubles, but frankly, no one in crisis wants your quick-fix feedback or to hear what others have dealt with unless the one suffering specifically asks for advice. There may be no concrete resolutions or conclusions to a hardship, regardless of the nature of the circumstances. Yes, you may have gone through a similar ordeal or know someone who did, but everyone's circumstances are different, and the predicament is about the ones currently experiencing the troublesome period, not you or anyone you know.

The affected person may require immediate hands-on support, talking through the emotional turmoil, or venting worries. They may need just five to ten minutes of your time to express their feelings. Give someone time to voice their doubts and concerns and, most importantly, listen. A crisis is about the person or family, and their problems should be at the heart of any conversation.

Reach out.

What Is Your Gift?

I firmly believe everyone has a personal, individual, special gift. I consider a gift a quality or trait that comes naturally and effortlessly, and everyone's gift is undoubtedly distinct and unique. You may already be aware of your goodwill service; however, some people may not fully recognize their specific, special talents. I have seen some characteristics unexpectedly and unknowingly arise when others are in crisis. It's worth thinking about.

What is your gift? Making a phone call to check in? Sending a note of concern? Cooking? Dropping off a gift card to a restaurant or grocery store? Grocery shopping? Running errands? Babysitting? Walking the dog? Pet-sitting? Laundry? Vacuuming or light housekeeping? Giving someone a ride to an appointment? Mowing the grass? Raking leaves? Shoveling snow? Sitting with someone so the caregiver can attend to something or just take a break? Do you have or know someone who may have medical equipment that someone can borrow? Can you help sort through routine bills, medical bills, or insurance forms? Can you help with technical issues with a cell phone, the internet, a television, a computer, etc.?

Consider another's hardship and extend help in an area that is most comfortable and easy for you.

Reach out.

What NOT To Say or Do When Someone is Going Through a Crisis

When a family, friend, neighbor, coworker, fellow church member, etc., is sandwiched in crisis, not only is it difficult to know what to say, but it can also be hard to know how to lend support. Often, those well-intentioned do not give any thought to the impact their words or actions may have on those in the throes of a dark period. I, as well as others I have spoken with over the years, have encountered some of the following statements and situations while experiencing a heartbreaking, troubling time. It is my hope that this section will be a useful guide of what not to say, what may be helpful to say, what not to do, and what may be helpful to do.

What Not to Say: *How are you?*

This is a natural question we all instinctively say that expresses genuine concern, but think about it. If you are aware of someone experiencing a hardship, how do you expect him or her to be doing? Those affected may be experiencing unsettling emotions, which may vary from one minute to the next—anxiety, hopelessness, fear, doubt, embarrassment, worry, etc. If you happen to ask this question, be prepared for the response, which may be dark and heavy, and you may be told more disturbing information than you may be comfortable hearing or knowing.

Instead: *I heard/know you are going through a trying time; I've been thinking about you.*

These statements show empathy and genuine concern, and the affected person will respond if he or she wishes to share feelings or details. If you have previously spoken with the affected person, another approach is to say, "How are you doing *today* [or *this week*]?" This phrase puts emphasis on *today* or *this week* rather than the recipient having to rehash the previous few days, weeks, etc.

What Not to Say: *Everything will be okay.*

Words of encouragement are meant to be positive and uplifting regardless of the nature of the ordeal. However, those dealing with challenges may barely be able to see clear skies beyond the hazy horizon. Being positive can feel like a major undertaking even though your words are intended to be optimistic.

Instead: *You are in my thoughts at this difficult time.*

You acknowledge the devastating period, and this statement expresses empathy. There is no correct, clear verbiage to express that a situation may improve, which may also be wishful.

What Not to Say: *How is AA (or other treatment/recovery program) going?*

This question shows sincerity, but the recipient may not want to share their progress. I have heard several people in treatment/recovery programs remark that they are uncomfortably interrogated, especially if they have not seen the one asking this question in quite a while. The affected person may not want to share his or her standing or discuss personal feelings or developments. A question such as this should not be the focus of a conversation when speaking with anyone in recovery. Treatment programs are individual, personal, and private, and the set plan may be for a short stint or continue for several years.

Instead: *I think about you often,* or *I hope things are going well for you.*

These remarks show empathy without being nosy, intrusive, brazen, or requiring an immediate response. Lending a nonjudgmental ear may be what is needed the most. Those affected will share if and when they are ready to do so. Be sensitive.

What Not to Say: *Let me know if you need anything.*

This is an open-ended statement when someone genuinely wants to help yet may be hesitant or unsure how to proceed. If the affected person is uneasy asking for or accepting assistance, this question can put the recipient in an awkward position. *What are they specifically asking? Should I give someone my grocery list? Should I request a meal?* Most often, they may not know what help might be beneficial, may withdraw, or perhaps may be so overwhelmed with the circumstance that it could be hard for them to even think straight, which is understandable.

Instead: Offer *specific* help. *I'm going to the grocery store tomorrow; text or email me your grocery list. I'm running errands on Tuesday; let me know what tasks I can complete for you (stopping by the library, post office, pet store, etc.). I'm home this weekend; I'd be happy to cut your grass on Saturday (or Sunday). I have some spare time on Monday; if you put your laundry on your front porch by 9 a.m., I'll wash and dry it and return it by 5 p.m. I'm free Wednesday morning; I'm happy to stop by and run the vacuum for you. I want to bring you dinner next week; let me know what night works best for you.*

Being *specific* in lending assistance makes it easy and comfortable for the recipient to respond and take you up on your offer. Even if you are already out running errands, you might call and leave a message or text the person, asking if there is anything you could pick up for them. Your offer may not be accepted, but reaching out is thoughtful and an act of kindness.

What Not to Say: *Let me know if you want a meal.*

The wording sounds like offering a meal is an afterthought even though the intention may have been sincere. This statement may put the recipient in a sensitive position to respond.

Instead: *I want to bring you dinner next week (or in the next week* *or two); let me know what night works best for you.*

Be *specific* in offering to bring someone a meal. It is *how* you ask that makes it easier for them to respond, "Thank you, next Wednesday would be very helpful." Often, when I believe someone could use a meal but does not want an organized meal team, I will call, text, or email the person stating, "I want to bring you dinner next Tuesday. Does that day work for you? I will leave the meal on your front porch at 6 p.m." Surprisingly, my approach has never been turned down, and I think most people appreciate the one-time or occasional offer.

What Not to Say: *I've got an extremely busy week, but if I can, I will try to bring you a meal.*

This statement may sound helpful, but honestly, it is not welcoming. Unintentionally, the emphasis is on the one making the statement (that he or she has a busy week) and not on the recipient struggling. The above remark may make the recipient feel like it is a hassle. No one should ever *try* to bring a meal or *try* to do something for those going through a distressing time. Those affected are dealing with a bona fide hardship and do not want to hear that you will *try* to bring dinner or *try* to complete another undertaking.

Instead: *I would like to bring you dinner next Tuesday. Is that a good night for you?*

Be specific in what you are offering. It is how you phrase the suggestion that is most welcoming and comfortable to the recipient.

What Not to Say: *What can I do?*

As sincere and heartfelt as this statement sounds, those in crisis may be apprehensive when asking for assistance or truly not know what is needed as they struggle with what is on their packed, shaky plate. It also puts an additional workload on the recipient to divvy up any needs that might be beneficial.

Instead: If you are unsure what direction of help may be needed, take it upon yourself to do what you feel may be supportive. There are countless ways to show support when exact needs may not be obvious or clear.

What Not to Say: *Let me know what I can do for you, but I don't vacuum or do yard work, and I'm allergic to cats.*

What? Do those rooted in crisis really want to call on this person for help? The person making this statement most likely had good intentions, but the phrasing is not welcoming.

Instead: Offer *specific* assistance, which you are comfortable handling. *Can I sit with _____ while you run an errand? Email me your grocery list, and I'll be happy to pick up what you need. Can I stop by Tuesday afternoon to walk your dog? Leave your laundry on the front porch in the morning, and I'll return it by 5 p.m. I understand your brother/sister is coming into town next week; can I pick him/her up at the airport?*

Offering *specific* help makes it easy and simple for the recipient to respond and take you up on your suggestion. Perhaps you are questioning exactly what assistance may be beneficial, but put yourself in someone else's shoes. What might help you if you were facing the same circumstances and challenges?

What Not to Say: *You need to be positive, You need to be strong,* or *Some people have it harder.*

Most people wrangling with a hardship may barely be able to wrap their heads around their current situation, and even though these statements are intended to be encouraging, reassuring, and uplifting, no one should be told how to feel. Everyone feels things differently.

Instead: *I was troubled to hear you are going through this. I am so sad this happened. I am here for you whenever you want to talk,* or *I can only imagine how difficult this time is for you.*

Realize that emotions and situations can be dark, intense, and massive. Often, a sympathetic ear is what is needed the most. Reach out. Be empathetic, compassionate, and supportive of someone's struggles.

What Not to Say: *My mother, uncle, cousin, etc., had (or went through) the same thing.*

No one going through a distressing time wants to hear what your mother, uncle, cousin, etc., had or went through. Even though the situation, diagnosis, or illness may be similar, everyone is different, and you should not compare circumstances. Outsiders may have a sense of insight into what another may be experiencing, which is understandable, but again, everyone is unique, and everyone feels things differently. As knowledgeable as someone may be about dealing with a comparable ordeal, this is not a statement a suffering person wants to hear (unless they request the information). The hardship occurring concerns the ones in crisis, not someone's mother, uncle, cousin, etc.

Instead: *I am here for you any time you want to talk.*

Reach out. Show compassion for someone's troubling period, and be mindful that the focus of any conversation should be on those dealing with a devastating time and not you, your family members, friends, and/or your experience.

What Not to Say: *So how long do the doctors say he/she has (when someone is nearing death)?*

Nothing along these lines should ever be said in the presence of anyone who is gravely ill. Even if the person appears to be resting or asleep, he or she most likely can hear what is being said. Research has shown that hearing is the last of the senses to go.

This statement was said by someone visiting John while he was at home in hospice—in his presence. I was absolutely appalled by this blunt, inappropriate question. John appeared to be napping, but no one should ever assume someone is sound asleep.

Instead: As tactless as this question is, should you feel the need to know someone's current health condition, it should be asked out of sight and hearing of the ill person. Any conversations of this nature should be held in another room. A family may find the current situation questionable, troubling, and heartbreaking, which may add unnecessary angst to their ongoing worries. Most often, a family will share the health status of their loved one if they are able, and if they do not, the conversation should be over.

What Not to Do: *Complain, complain, complain—about anything.*

During John's six-month illness, I heard many people complain about very trivial issues—my doctor was forty-five minutes late to see me today, my flight was delayed an hour, there was an accident on the interstate, and I sat in traffic for thirty minutes, and the grocery store was out of rolls that were on special this week. Really? No one dealing with a crisis wants to hear minute, petty remarks like these. I would have given anything to have some of these small, minor annoyances rather than living day in and day out with the heartache and stress of caring for my critically ill husband. Others complained about something their child, sibling, spouse, parent, friend, boss, etc., had said or done to upset them. My husband was terminally ill, with no realistic chance of survival, and I did not want to hear a complaint someone had with their spouse or anyone else who would live to see another day, week, month, or much longer.

Instead: *Don't complain.*

No one wants to hear grievances of trivial situations or relationships, especially those who are deeply netted in a tumultuous period. Minor gripes seem inconsequential when enduring a challenging ordeal or major hardship. Even several years after John's death, I am very touchy when I hear others grumble. There are so many people who are dealing with major difficulties, and minor gripes seem insignificant. Perhaps I am a little more sensitive than others after going through a heartbreaking period.

What Not to Do: *Avoid someone hurting, an ill person, or a troubled family regardless of the circumstance or setting.*

Many people are so uneasy being around someone going through a tragic ordeal that they avoid the person and/or family. Many people do not know what to say, so they dodge the uncomfortable situation. There is no question that some predicaments or settings can feel unsettling. Perhaps some scenarios may make people uneasily aware of their own troubles or mortality. Others have warily hinted that they do not want to carry the memory of their loved one or dear friend in a treatment facility, hospital, jail cell, or on his or her deathbed. Again, it's not about how uncomfortable you may feel; it is about the person and their family. Do not shy away from anyone who is in a painful spot.

Instead: Comfort and support can be soothing, and it speaks volumes. A visit shows you care and can be meaningful. If visits are welcome, make the time to pay a visit, and if possible, don't go empty-handed. The visit does not need to be long. A friendly smile, a hug, or a squeeze of the hand while saying, "I've been thinking about you," is all you need to do.

What Not to Do: *If privacy has been requested, do not show up at the hospital, treatment facility, nursing home, or the person's home unannounced, even if you are a family member, close friend, coworker, or neighbor.*

You may feel the urge to pop in to support someone who is in the hospital, treatment facility, nursing home, or at home, but when privacy is noted, outsiders should be respectful of boundaries. The family may need private, tranquil time to be with their loved one without disruptions. Those facing difficulties or overseeing day-to-day responsibilities may feel emotionally and physically drained, brokenhearted, stressed, and/or overwhelmed.

From the beginning of John's diagnosis, I asked for privacy, and 90 percent of the time, my request was honored. I was very protective of John, and I also wanted private time to be with and care for him.

The doorbell often rang at the most inopportune times; I need not say more. I later learned several people were upset and offended when we did not answer the door, knowing my children and I were at home. Emotionally, we were not up to greeting anyone, regardless of who it was. I wish others were understanding of our constant, painful, roller-coaster emotions and daily struggles that resulted in the need for privacy.

Instead: Be sensitive. Respect requests for privacy or boundaries. As I mentioned earlier, a family in crisis may wish to leave a note on the hospital/treatment facility door or their home front door requesting privacy. If you find this to be the case, you may want to drop a card of concern in the mail, in the mailbox, or at their front door, stating that you are thinking of them and requesting they reach out, noting your contact information if and when they need it. Depending on the situation, you can leave what you brought at the nurses' station, at the facility's reception desk, or at the family's front door, and let the family know that you dropped something off.

What Not to Do: *Repeatedly call, text, or email the suffering person or family or drop by unannounced.*

Yes, you may want to get the latest update on the situation, but repeated communication can be overwhelming. Whether or not someone asked for privacy, those affected should not be bombarded with constant phone calls, texts, or emails; space may be important to grasp or handle what is currently on their plate. Do not pile on any additional chaos.

Instead: There is a fine line between reaching out to lend a helping hand and inconspicuously prying or meddling. It can be hard, but outsiders often need to take a step or two back and provide a little space for those struggling. As long as they know they can contact you if needed, that is what is important.

What Not to Do: *Offer unsolicited feedback or uninvited solutions to another's hardships.*

It is understandably difficult to sit back and watch someone who's navigating troubling adversities and situations; this can be a delicate and sensitive area. Pay attention to what is being said without giving unsolicited recommendations or answers to their problems. You may feel the need to offer sensible solutions, but the affected person may just need a sympathetic ear or a trusting shoulder to lean on, not outside feedback (unless you are specifically asked).

Instead: Be mindful of when to speak up and when to remain silent. Often, a nonjudgmental ear is needed. Can you be that person who shows up, listens, and is just *there* for those in crisis?

What Not to Do: *When delivering a meal, do not bring food in breakable, special dishes, or a container that needs to be returned.*

Yes, the meal may look more attractive in a decorative casserole dish, but those in crisis do not have the time to keep up with who brought what container and return it to the correct person.

Instead: Food items should be delivered in disposable foil pans, plastic containers, or Zip Top bags, well-labeled with the item, cooking or heating instructions, the name of the person who prepared it, and the date. Disposable containers make cleanup effortless and can be found at most grocery stores or big-box stores for a few dollars.

What Not to Do: *Nothing.*

Not reaching out is hurtful and inexcusable. Many people are uncomfortable and do not know what to say or do, so they do nothing rather than risk doing the wrong thing. Everyone will face a challenging time or crisis at some point, and most likely, you would want support if the roles were reversed. Try to imagine yourself in someone else's shoes.

Instead: If you are uncertain or uneasy because of their situation, you can let them know you are there for them by leaving a voice message on their phone, dropping off a thinking-of-you note at their front door, or mailing a note of concern. The affected person or family can contact you if they need something. Do not feel offended if you do not get a response; those struggling may not have the time or strength to respond or even ask for help. So long as you make the effort to reach out, it shows you care, and that is what is important. There is no excuse for remaining silent when others are experiencing a trying ordeal. There is always some way to lend support when needs are not readily apparent. Those going through a trying period should be showered with countless acts of kindness. Offer support in an area that is easy and comfortable for you.

What Not to Do: *Slack off on commitments.*

If you offered to deliver a meal, complete a task, etc., show up, be on time, and fulfill the commitment. Those dealing with hardship are counting on your pledge, and when you are late, forget, or do not show up, it can add additional snags to an already overwhelming day. I know of a family contending with health issues who received meals several days a week, and the person who volunteered to bring dinner one night never showed up, and the family had to scramble to pull together a meal with whatever they had on hand. Yes, unexpected setbacks can arise that may be out of anyone's control, and if this happens, be sure to call to say you are running late or will have to reschedule so no one is left in the dark.

Several times, I scheduled an appointment when someone offered to sit with John, and the person was thirty minutes to an hour late. As much as I appreciated someone staying with him so I could leave the house briefly, it was not worth it when the person was late, and I had to rearrange my plans.

Instead: *Follow through on your commitment.*

Those in crisis are counting on your commitment when you offered to do something for them. Do not leave anyone hanging who may be depending on you. Show up and be on time.

PART 4

Helping Others Following a Crisis

Following a stormy ordeal or difficult health issue, it is important to stay in touch and provide ongoing support to those suffering. In fact, this is the time when family and friends are needed more than ever; I cannot emphasize this enough. Regardless of the circumstances of the crisis, awkwardness and discomfort should not stop anyone from reaching out and responding to those who have gone through a tumultuous ordeal and who may be struggling with the aftermath. The feelings of uneasiness and discomfort need to change.

This section focuses on how to help someone when a crisis is over. These suggestions can be tailored to the specific trauma your friend or loved one went through. There is no question that words can be hard to find when encountering those who have endured a hardship; however, realize that actions often speak louder than words. The assumption that those hurting are fine after one, two, three, or even many years later is wishful. Those who experienced a traumatic time may have many invisible, hidden wounds that may never heal.

The initial year following a tumultuous period or death may be a complete blur for many people. All the *firsts* (Valentine's Day, Mother's Day, Father's Day, birthdays, anniversaries, etc.) seem to be the most difficult. I have heard many people remark that holidays following a crisis continue to be tough many years later. An unspeakable ordeal or the death of a loved one may be hard to process, and everyone deals with a tragic situation in their own way and in their own time. A crisis can be crushing, disabling, and life-changing. There is no established timeline when moving forward, and the pain and devastation may remain present many years later.

After listening to others who have gone through a distressing time, the following suggestions may be helpful to reach out, respond, and provide support following any crisis.

The Darkness of Death

The world stops for a short time when someone passes away, then starts up again and keeps moving on, but not for those who have lost a loved one.

Death

Everyone will experience the death of a loved one or someone with whom they had a relationship. Grief is indescribable, and emotions run the gamut from depression, hopelessness, and despair to despondency, anguish, and fear of the future. Some people may heal quickly following a loss, while others may never rebound. Be mindful that there may be nothing you can say or do to make someone feel better following a death, yet being present and acknowledging the painful time survivors went through and may continue to endure means a lot. Survivors need ongoing support as they process their sorrowful time.

Recognize that significant dates such birthdays, anniversaries, and holidays can be extremely difficult following the death of someone special. Grief does not wane and may linger for a long time. Continue to reach out to those mourning a death. No one ever forgets or gets over the loss of a loved one.

Reach out.

Death of a Child

Anyone having experienced the death of a child, regardless of the age or circumstance, is something for which no one is ever prepared. No one should ever have to go through the emotional toll of losing a child, but unfortunately, it happens too often. Whatever you can do to show support is vital as the survivor(s) attempt to cope with the tragedy. No one ever loses sight or fully recovers from the loss of someone dear, especially a child. Touching base should not fade or vanish following a death. Be understanding and compassionate of someone's loss.

Reach out.

Death by Suicide

Support is critical to those grappling with the loss of a family member, friend, coworker, neighbor, etc., by suicide. There may be nothing you can say or do to help those left behind, but acknowledging the pain and stating you are there for them while keeping them in your thoughts and prayers is essential. Touching base with the survivor(s) should not diminish once the funeral is over. The idea of the survivor bouncing back is hopeful. Offer your kindness with the ideas listed throughout this book.

Reach out.

Understanding Emotions and Ways to Offer Support Following a Tragic Period

A crisis can be devastating and difficult to process regardless of what the circumstance may have been. Following a tragic period or death, the shadow of despair and/or grief can be massively dark, and although the murky time may fade as times passes, it truly never disappears.

Be Sensitive

Be mindful that those having experienced a tumultuous time or the death of someone special process the adversity in their own way and in their own time. How someone copes following any crisis is personal, private, and individual, and their feelings and actions should never be minimized or judged. The waves of emotions can be exhausting, painful, and complicated. Too many times, those hurting are left alone to work through and deal with the aftermath of their battle, and connecting with others may provide the necessary support in the healing process.

Some people withdraw from others as they sort through their feelings, while some people find comfort in inviting the world to share in their heartache. In either case, reach out and let those hurting know you are thinking of them. The rippling effects of wavering emotions may continue for a long, long time once the crisis is over. Empathy and compassion are imperative.

Do not shy away from talking about the painful period or the deceased when speaking with the family, friend, coworker, neighbor, etc. A big fear of many survivors following a tragedy or death is that the immediate family or the deceased's memory will disappear and be forgotten. Many people find comfort in hearing recollections or stories of the affected person or the departed. They may tear up when discussing what they went through or their loved one, which is understandable. Remaining silent when you run into those who experienced a hardship is hurtful and truthfully, unjustifiable; avoiding what occurred should never occur. Acknowledge the agonizing time or loss. Follow the hurting person's lead, and use your judgment. If you find discussing the situation or the deceased too emotional and painful, note how troublesome you can imagine this time is and move the conversation on to something else.

Be sensitive to the conversation. Words can be hard to find following any dark period. If someone has experienced a miscarriage, you should not talk on and on about your baby, child, or grandchild. If someone has a child who encountered depression, you should not talk about how wonderful your child or grandchild is. If someone has lost a parent, you should not talk about how you celebrated Mother's Day or Father's Day with your parent. If someone has lost a spouse, you should not talk about how you and your partner are spending your anniversary or the fabulous vacation you have planned. This is common sense, yet comments continue to be made without thoughtful consideration of those who may be emotionally hurting.

When a crisis first occurs, family and friends are most often front and center, providing comfort, support, or other backing. When the hardship continues for any length of time or ultimately ends, surprisingly, the concern frequently tapers off and dwindles down as time goes on. This may leave the recipient feeling confused, heavyhearted, and alone. Continue to reach out to those following the aftermath of any tumultuous circumstance. Connecting and checking in on those who have gone through a troubling time or a loss should never lessen when the traumatic period has ended.

Reach out.

Providing Meals/Food

Following a tumultuous ordeal or death, meals can be a tremendous help for those attempting to move forward as they begin to tackle the healing process. Family and friends may be in town to provide needed assistance immediately following a crisis or to attend planned funeral services. Often, the last thing those hurting can consider is what to serve when mealtime rolls around. First and foremost, it is important to determine if meals would be helpful and when they would be most needed. A family may already be overloaded with food, so you do not want to deliver items that are not needed. A meal team or meal train may be beneficial to help a family as they process a distressing time. An online meal signup site is a wonderful outreach for others to volunteer to deliver food that suits their schedule.

If food is welcome, find out how many a meal should serve and if there are any food dislikes or allergies. Items should be in disposable containers with any refrigerator or cooking instructions clearly noted. You might also want to provide a few paper products to make the serving and clean-up process effortless.

A few suggestions to lighten someone's load following a traumatic time are below.

Breakfast/Brunch: Providing breakfast/brunch items would be appreciated anytime and may be especially helpful the day before, on the morning of, or even the day following a memorial service. The days surrounding a funeral can be a busy, sad, and fragile time, and having breakfast/brunch provided can lighten someone's load, especially if out-of-town guests or family are around. Breakfast items can be dropped off the day before or early on the morning of the service so the family only needs to heat or bake the main dish and set out the other items so guests can serve themselves.

Lunch: Delivering fixings for lunch can lighten a daily undertaking. Another option is to pick up a variety of already-prepared sandwiches or lunch items from a grocery store or restaurant.

Dinner: Any type of entrée item with a vegetable, starch, salad, rolls, and dessert would be appreciated on the night of a visitation, funeral service, celebration of life, or even a day or two later. Delivering dinner following a funeral might be welcome following a long emotional day, especially if there are out-of-town family visiting or guests stopping in.

If you find providing a meal a bit overwhelming, partner up with a friend to make the task more manageable. If you do not cook or do not have time to prepare a meal, picking up an already-prepared dinner from a grocery store or restaurant, dropping off a restaurant gift card, or dropping off a VISA-type gift card are wonderful options. Frozen food items are an excellent outreach too, assuming the family has freezer space. Again, ask. Do what is most comfortable and easy for you. You can also combine a homemade meal with a few store-bought items.

If you are questioning what type of food to bring, give some thought to your favorite recipes. You may have select go-to dinners that others have enjoyed. Depending on the time of year, spring and summer call for light, simple, foods such as fresh fruits and vegetables and grilled dishes, while fall and winter draw more hearty, comfort foods such as casseroles, soups, chili, pasta, etc. Perhaps your quiche, blueberry muffins, or famous chocolate chip cookies are your best-loved recipes; you can just complete the menu with other food items.

A thoughtful gesture when providing a meal is to contact the person or family a day or two ahead and ask if there is anything at the grocery store you can pick up. Since you are already stopping by, it's easy to pick up something and drop off the items at the same time.

Depending on the situation, an individual or a family may need meals for a week or two or on a regular basis for an extended period. As I mentioned earlier, an online meal signup site is easy to set up and is a supportive opportunity for volunteers to choose a date to deliver dinner on a day that suits his or her schedule. Relevant details should be included on the link, such as how many people a meal should serve, food dislikes or allergies, the recipient's address and phone number, the best time to deliver dinner, if a cooler is available, etc. A cooler can be left on the recipient's front porch or by a side door to simplify drop-offs, and it also maintains privacy if desired. Meals delivered Mondays, Wednesdays, and Fridays or Tuesdays and Thursdays work well for most people.

If the mother, father, or caregiver of a young family has passed away, you can approach the surviving parent to find out if he or she would welcome meals for several months until a routine is established and life begins to settle down. Be sure to extend meal signups for additional months if needed. Restaurant gift cards are helpful, too, to show support. Keep in mind that the surviving parent and/or the immediate family has a lot on their plate, and anything you can do to lighten their responsibilities is an act of kindness and a true blessing at a sad time.

If you do not cook or time restricts you from providing a homecooked dinner, a meal delivery service is an option. A gift certificate for a delivery service can be purchased online, emailed, printed out, and delivered to the recipient. Those affected can then order food from a restaurant of their choice following a long, tiring day.

A few days following John's death, a friend texted me asking what night that week would be most helpful for her to bring dinner. She knew I had out-of-town family staying with me for a week. Note that she did not ask if I *wanted* or *needed* a meal; she asked *what night* she could bring dinner. Asking in this way made me feel comfortable accepting her offer and was much appreciated at a sorrowful time.

I received a fully-cooked ham from a long-time friend of John's who lived out-of-state and was unable to attend his funeral. With the number of relatives in town for the services, the ham provided dinner one night and sandwiches for lunch the next couple of days. Local friends delivered a fresh fruit basket and homemade quiches that we had the morning of the memorial service. These items were helpful with the number of family members staying with me, and it lifted a lot of weight off my shoulders.

Reach out.

Funeral Home Visitations, Memorial Services, and Celebrations of Life

There is no question that funeral home visitations, memorial services, celebrations of life gatherings, or any other end-of-life event can be uncomfortable. Think of the family who has suffered a tremendous loss. Your appearance lends essential emotional support to those mourning the death of a loved one. Take the time to personally speak to the grieving survivors at the service(s). If you have never met the immediate family, introduce yourself and let them know how you were connected to the deceased. Speaking with the family will most likely be brief as they will be busy greeting other visitors. A simple embrace or gentle touch on the arm or shoulder and stating, "I've been thinking about you and your family," is all that needs to be said. There is no need to fixate on specific wordage to offer condolences. No one can remedy a tumultuous time or mend a broken heart. Your presence speaks volumes.

If end of life services are planned, you should attend at least one or all the gatherings if you are able. I was surprised by the number of people who came to John's services to express sympathy and extend support to my family and me. Local and out-of-state friends attended the events to convey their condolences. I was deeply moved by those who came; it meant the world to me that people took time out of their day to stop by. I may have only spoken to some visitors for a minute or two, but it truly touched my family and me, and I will always remember those who attended. Looking into the church sanctuary to see a group of my coworkers, some of whom did not know John well or had never met him, is an image I will never forget.

Reach out.

Guest Book

It is important to sign the guest book if one is provided at the funeral home visitation, memorial service, or celebration of life. Emotions are high and unsettling, and it is meaningful to the family to look back through the visitor's log to remember who attended. Your name and address should be clearly written if the family needs the information later. If you do not know the immediate family, make a note about how you are connected to the deceased. For the immediate family, this takes the mystery out of seeing an unfamiliar name. *N/C* noted after a visitor's name signifies *no card*. When this notation is written, the family does not need to send a note to the visitor(s), thanking them for attending the service(s).

Reach out.

Wordage—Loss, Passed, Death

Everyone has a varied viewpoint when hearing or using the words *loss*, *passed*, or *death*. You might give some thought to which word(s) you are most comfortable using; these words are certainly interchangeable. Whatever words you use are personal, but it's worth thinking about.

Loss. Some survivors do not like the word *loss*; someone didn't lose their keys or wallet; a person died. The word *loss* refers to something misplaced, but it also refers to bereavement.

Passed. Some people cringe when hearing the word *passing* or *passed*. The word *pass* can refer to a cut in a canyon or going by something, but *pass* also refers to succumbing to death.

Death clearly means the end of life.

Be mindful when sending a note or speaking with a survivor, and use the word(s) with which you are most comfortable. I prefer loss (which does not mean my husband was lost and thus missing, but I lost my husband to death) or death.

Reach out.

Wordage—Sorry

Sorry is a common, overused word and can have a complicated connotation. The word *sorry* can relate to sadness, grief, or sympathy, showing deep remorse, but it can also be an expression of apology. Saying *sorry* is like you are excusing yourself for something you did and now regret, and truthfully, the hardship another experienced was obviously out of your control.

How you use the word is important. Those coping may be piercingly sensitive when outsiders address the situation. Saying, "I'm sorry about what happened," and "I'm sorry for your loss" are dead-end statements to which the recipient's response may only be "thank you." A more approachable wording is "I'm sorry you went through this devastating time," or "I'm sorry that you have lost _____," which puts the focus on the recipient and the difficult time. Alternative wording is this: "I was troubled to learn/hear of your tragic ordeal," or "I was saddened to learn/hear of _____'s death."

Reach out.

What to Say Following a Traumatic Ordeal or Death

Conversations can be extremely uncomfortable and awkward. Do not dwell on how uneasy you may feel when addressing the difficult circumstances, but think of those who just went through a painful time. Death *is* heavy, death *is* uncomfortable, and tragic situations are just as weighty. Too often people search for the correct wording to extend warmth and sympathy, and truthfully, there are no magic words. Acknowledge the pain and realize that no one can remedy an unfortunate period or restore a broken heart, yet expressing compassion can be heartwarming to those hurting.

Suggested dialogue:

I've been thinking about you and your family.

I was sad to learn what you went through; please know you and your family have been in my thoughts and prayers.

I was heartbroken to hear of your difficulties; you are in my thoughts and prayers.

There are no adequate words at this difficult time; please know I'm thinking of you.

I'm here to listen if you need me.

If you are still at a total loss, being honest is appropriate. *I'm at a loss for words for what you have gone through,* or *I'm at a loss for words in the death of _____.* Your sincerity is genuine and heartfelt and will be appreciated.

Go out of your way to speak to those who endured a tumultuous period or who may be mourning the death of someone dear; not addressing the adversity is like the circumstance or deceased did not matter or exist. Even if you attended the visitation, memorial service, and/or celebration of life gathering and you later run into the family, confront the tragic time, whether it's a week, a month, or many years later. No one ever forgets what they went through or the death of a loved one. Skirting a troubling ordeal can be hurtful for those attempting to heal.

Reach out.

Sympathy Cards

A sympathy card is a sincere way to extend condolences and lets the survivor(s) know they are being thought of at a sorrowful time. The impact of a simple card is immeasurable. Even if a sympathy card has a printed verse, take the time to write a personal note expressing your solace. Any fond memory you have of the deceased is notable and can be uplifting to those grieving. Your remembrance may be new and special to them.

I have heard several people express their disappointment in receiving a text or email of sympathy, which, truthfully, is thoughtless and cold. Sending a text or email to initially acknowledge the loss is fine, but you should follow up with a personalized note. It only takes a minute to pick up a sympathy card and handwrite words of condolences. A blank note expressing your condolences is always appropriate too.

Be mindful of the spelling of the deceased's name; using incorrect spelling of the departed's name is very impersonal at an already emotional time for the family.

A sympathy card does not need to be sent immediately but should be sent within a few weeks. Three to four weeks after John died, I received several notes from people who stated they needed time to put their thoughts of sympathy into words. If you know the family of the deceased, a sympathy card sent separately to them is a must.

In particular, I received one sympathy card following John's death from someone whose name I did not know, yet I recognized the return address, several streets away in the neighborhood. The card included a handwritten note that she was sad to learn of John's death. The neighbor wrote that she regularly saw John while she was out walking, and he always smiled and said hello. This person stated that she would miss seeing his friendly face on her daily walks. Unaware of these occurrences, I was truly touched that she took the time to reach out to me. I assume the neighbor had seen John's obituary in the newspaper. Her kind note meant a lot to me.

Reach out.

Memorial Funds

If a contribution to a memorial fund or a specific organization is suggested and/or in lieu of flowers following a death, give a donation if you are able. Honoring the deceased in this way means a lot to the grieving family. The contribution can be in any amount. Be sure to specify that the contribution is in memory of the deceased and ask that the family be notified of the donation by providing their name and address. This should be done within three to four weeks following a death.

Reach out.

Children, Teens, or Young Adults Coping with Loss

When a child, teen, or young adult suffers a loss, emotions can range from heartache and sadness to confusion and fearfulness, not to mention complicated feelings at their age. It is not uncommon for families and friends to lose sight of young people's developing emotional mechanisms. Special attention needs to be given to any young person who may be attempting to understand or make any kind of sense of the loss. Grief counseling may be helpful in the healing process.

For a child under eighteen, sharing a special memory or a personal thought and a small gift may console the child as they go through a somber, confusing, and life-changing time. The gift might be a stuffed animal, toy, jewelry, music box, journal, etc., that the child can hold onto in memory of their loved one; the gift should be age-appropriate. A picture frame makes a thoughtful gift for the child to insert a photo of their loved one.

Reach out.

The Time Immediately Following a Difficult Ordeal or Death

When a difficult time is over, continue to stay in touch with those affected. Those impacted never forget what they went through, producing puzzling feelings when all outside communications stop. Support should be ongoing and is critical for someone's healthy emotional wellness. Do not loiter on the sidelines or disappear.

Perhaps you are a coworker, neighbor, or part of a particular group. Can you and the others combine efforts and do something special to acknowledge someone's hardship or loss? Donations can be collected for a specific cause, charity, or organization, planting a tree or perennial shrub in honor of the deceased, or another way of recognizing the distressing ordeal and/or memorializing the deceased.

Reach out.

Crisis or Grief Assistance/Counseling

Counseling may be vital following a crisis or death. There are many counselors available to meet privately or in a group setting. Many sessions may be needed in the healing process.

Families and friends tend to come together following a crisis or death; however, this is not always the case. Some relationships cannot withstand a devastating period. Circumstances and grief can drive a wedge between relationships and connections for a number of reasons.

Many inspirational books are readily available, covering mental health issues, addictions, substance or physical abuse, cancer, hospice, death, suicide, grief, etc. Although it may be a kind gesture to give someone an encouraging book on moving forward, be sensitive and selective in presenting the appropriate resource.

Following John's death, I received several books on bereavement from well-intentioned people. These resources highlighted a widow's feelings—from being alone to finances to adjusting to a new lifestyle—but they did not offer the kind of comfort I hoped for. I have yet to read a book on grief that offered real life comfort and relatable viewpoints as my experience was different than anyone else's because it was mine.

Reach out.

Additional Suggestions

Reaching out to those having gone through a trying time with empathy, compassion, and simple acts of kindness is thoughtful and immeasurable.

More Thoughtful Ways to Lend Support

If you are close to those who experienced a challenging time or loss or are aware that those affected do not have a lot of backing, there are additional thoughtful ways to reach out. Your relationship with those hurting should be your guide, and it's important to lend support in an area you are most comfortable handling.

You can offer to assist in writing thank-you notes following a crisis or death. Try to make the best of a somber time by getting together in the morning for coffee, at noon for lunch, at happy hour with a bottle of wine and snacks, or in the evening for dinner or dessert.

If organization or finance comes easy for you, offer to assist in sorting through routine and medical bills or insurance paperwork or accompany someone to meetings with attorneys, financial advisors, the Department of Motor Vehicles, court appointments, etc.

Perhaps technology is effortless for you. Your guidance in purchasing or changing cell phones, televisions, iPads, computers, internet services, electronic problems, etc., may be valuable.

If you are aware that someone needs to go through the deceased's clothes or personal effects and is having a hard time doing so, offer to assist. This can be a very sensitive undertaking. Your suggestion may be turned down, but you don't know unless you ask.

Lend assistance with anything someone may not be able to manage alone (e.g., dropping off a vehicle to be serviced, bringing boxes down from the attic, rearranging furniture, moving deck furniture, replacing a light bulb in a high-ceiling foyer or garage, dropping off unneeded things at a local thrift store, taking items to a recycling center or the dump, etc.).

Reach out.

Pick Up the Phone

One of the easiest ways to reach out to those who have faced a hurdle or dark adversity is to call them to check in—often. Hearing a friendly voice means a lot even if the person does not answer the phone; a voice message of concern speaks volumes. Continue to touch base for a year or two, depending on the situation and your relationship with the person. Too often, those hurting are left alone to cope with their unsettling emotions, which may feel extremely lonely and detached.

I have heard many people remark that they are bad at keeping in touch even when things in life are going well, whether it is connecting with family members, long-time friends, neighbors, etc. It only takes a few minutes to check in; a phone call is a simple, uncomplicated means to stay in touch. Pick up the phone and bring a little sunshine to another's day.

Reach out.

Invitations

An act of kindness is as simple as asking anyone hurting to join you for coffee, breakfast, lunch, happy hour, dinner, a movie, a local event, a social get-together, a holiday gathering, etc. Those affected are most likely sitting at home day after day, night after night, and may enjoy a little friendly conversation and time away from the house. If possible, try to make frequent plans to help take someone's mind off their sadness. Be sure to acknowledge that they have been in your thoughts. Understand that the pain others may feel can be massive, and realize that is okay. Use your judgment when making conversation when you meet up.

Do not feel offended if someone is not up for getting together. Be mindful that those hurting may be going through a rough spot, and continue to touch base for at least several months or possibly longer. Those brokenhearted may need time to process the difficult situation and a little uninterrupted space.

Reach out.

Inclusion

When invited to an event of mutual friends or acquaintances, invite someone who has gone through a dark period to join you. If possible, pick them up. Most people feel more comfortable attending get-togethers with another person or couple. Do not feel riled if the invitation to join you is declined. Continue to touch base through phone calls, emails, and cards.

In a social setting, make a point to speak to or sit by someone who appears to be alone. No one truly knows what someone has faced or gone through; a short, friendly conversation can brighten and possibly highlight another's dreary day.

Reach out.

When the Waves of Emotions Continue

No one should ever feel alone, isolated, or forgotten when a crisis ends.

Sensitive Dates and Holidays

Important dates are never forgotten and are always in the hearts of those who have wrestled through a tumultuous time or lost someone dear. Remember specific dates such as the affected person's or the deceased's birthday or date of death, wedding day, or other memorable point in time with a phone call, a thinking-of-you note, flowers, etc. You may want to mark relevant dates on your calendar as a reminder to reach out. Connecting with empathy and compassion is meaningful and can brighten a gloomy day.

I find the word *anniversary* somewhat troublesome when referring to the yearly calendar date of a troubling period or loss. I relate *anniversary* with a time of joyful celebration, and there is no happy observance when marking the first, second, third year, etc., following a horrific ordeal or death. *Remembrance* seems to be a more appropriate word.

Holidays may be extremely difficult for many people. The stress, anxiety, sadness, and uneasiness of a holiday may be emotionally painful and unbearable. The rest of the world is celebratory during festive times, but not for those who have wrangled with a crisis. The empty chair at the kitchen table may be too much to bear and the massive daily absence of someone dear. Annual traditions may be gone or never be the same; sensitivity should be center stage.

Reach out.

Individuals Having Gone Through or Completed a Recovery Program

For anyone who has gone through or completed a recovery program (eating disorder, drug, alcohol, or sex addiction, emotional and/or physical abuse, anger management, etc.), support should be ongoing. Often a nonjudgmental ear or a solid shoulder to lean on is what is needed the most. What can you do to support and encourage someone attempting to move forward in the healing process?

Reach out.

Show Up, Be There, Be Present, and Most Importantly, Listen

Show up, be there, be present, emotionally, and physically, listen, lend support, and offer comfort to those who have scuffled through a hardship or suffered a loss.

A few months after John died, I was out to dinner with a friend who said, "You are the first of my friends to lose a spouse. Honestly, I do not know what to do to help you going forward." Her remarks took me off guard. After considering her comments, I responded, "Thank you. I truly don't know either." It was then when I realized my friend was there for me, and I appreciated her honesty. She cared; she was there, present, and ready to support me. Bottom line? I knew I had to face an unanticipated, unwanted path alone, and the support from others made the new journey a bit more bearable.

Show up. Be there. Be present. Listen.

Reach out.

Just Do

Take it upon yourself to do anything you think may be helpful following a difficult time. Do not sit back and wait to be asked for assistance as most likely those hurting may feel overwhelmed with the aftermath or may not have the time or strength to ask for help. Those hurting may pull back and need some time and a little space to process what occurred. They may be emotionally and physically spent and find it hard to get back into life itself. Know that just getting through the day may be a major, strained effort. Show empathy and compassion with acts of kindness. Your actions will be appreciated. Just do.

Reach out.

Lift Up

Whatever you can do to lift up those who have experienced a trying time or who may be mourning is a thoughtful gesture. As I have mentioned several times, reach out in an area that is most comfortable for you. There are endless ways to raise someone's spirits. Be creative, and think outside the box. Your deeds will be heartwarming and are genuine acts of kindness.

Soon after John died, I mentioned to a friend that I felt like dark clouds were hanging over me. A toilet overflowed raw sewage several times (unbeknownst at the time, a tree root had grown into a major pipe, causing the backup), I had major car problems when I was out of town, experiencing a dead battery at the most inopportune time, and I had to make the difficult decision to put my cat down after he was unexpectedly diagnosed with liver cancer. The trying times seemed to go on and on; I just could not seem to get a break. Several days later, I found a gift bag at my front door from my friend with a note: *Here's a little something when there are dark clouds*. Inside the bag was a bright, colorful umbrella that brought a smile to my face and warmed my heart. I always think of her when it is raining, and I pull out the cheerful umbrella.

      Reach out.

Acknowledgment

Anyone who has gone through a crisis may continue to experience a whirlwind of mixed emotions and often struggles with the aftermath. Be mindful that the time following a hardship is when family and friends are needed the most. I cannot emphasize enough the importance of acknowledging someone's distressing or painful period. Yes, it can be very uncomfortable and awkward to address circumstances that may have been dark, disturbing, unthinkable, or foreign, yet ignoring the trying time is thoughtless and, frankly, inexcusable. The tragedy is most likely at the center of the affected person's thoughts each and every day. Too many times, outsiders shun, dodge, disappear, or turn their backs on those who have dealt with hardship or death, maybe not intentionally, but perhaps feeling ill at ease or apprehensive.

 When a circumstance goes unacknowledged, those brokenhearted often feel like their problems are of no great importance or their loved ones do not matter or even exist. It is unjustifiable to sweep someone's stormy period under the rug or look the other way, especially if you were aware of their battles. It means the world to those hurting when others address the hardship by reaching out with empathy, compassion, and acts of kindness.

      Reach out.

Keep In Mind

It's at troubling times when support is needed the most.

It's Not About You

Following a trying time or death, those directly affected often feel heartbroken and confused when others neglect to acknowledge or listen to their distressing period. Many times, outsiders unintentionally want to offer quick-fix feedback, but frankly, those having gone through a crisis do not want to hear how you would have dealt with a similar situation unless you are specifically asked for advice. Yes, you may have gone through an identical or similar ordeal, but everyone's circumstances are different, and the predicament is about them, not you.

Those affected may need to talk through the emotional turmoil, vent, or convey their feelings for five to ten minutes. Give someone time to voice their worries and listen. The outcome is about the person or the immediate family, and their concerns should be the focus of any conversation. Set aside your feelings, thoughts, and advice; lend support, and console those trying to make sense of and process their dark time as they attempt to move forward.

Reach out.

What Is Your Gift?

I am a firm believer that everyone has a gift, special quality, or attribute that comes naturally. Sometimes these gifts are not obvious but may unexpectedly appear and can be a true blessing for anyone who has faced challenges.

What is your gift? Can you send a thinking-of-you note? Can you pick up the phone to touch base and check in with a nonjudgmental ear? Can you deliver a hearty meal? Can you drop off a gift card for a restaurant or grocery store? Can you pick up something at the drugstore or chain store? Can you walk the dog? Can you babysit? Can you take someone's car in for routine maintenance? Can you vacuum or do laundry? Can you cut the grass? Can you walk alongside someone who is attempting to get back into life? Provide support in an area that is easy and comfortable for you.

Reach out.

What NOT to Say or Do Following a Crisis

Once a crisis is over, regardless of how it may have ended, it can be difficult to know what to say and hard to know how to provide support. Often, those with good intentions do not consider the impact of their words or actions. I, and others I have spoken with, have encountered some of the following statements and situations. It is my hope that this section can be a useful guide for how to approach those in the aftermath of a turbulent period.

What Not to Say: *Is Susie still in counseling or rehab [for alcoholism, drug addiction, an eating disorder, mental health problems, relationship issues, etc.]?*

How long do you expect Susie will be in counseling?

When do you think Susie will be released from the treatment facility?

Yes, you may want to get the latest update, but these statements can put someone on the spot. They may be emotionally distraught or prefer not to share their latest accounts.

Instead: *I think about Susie often.*

This is all that needs to be said and shows concern without being too personal or intrusive. The family will respond further if they choose to discuss current developments.

What Not to Say: *You are young; you can try again (following a miscarriage).*

Well, at least you already have a healthy child.

It was probably for the best.

A miscarriage is a tremendous loss for anyone. Hopes and dreams for a baby and the family's anticipated future were shattered. It's devastating and indescribable. Even if you've experienced it, everyone's feelings and responses are different.

Instead: *I was sad to learn of your miscarriage. I am thinking of you and keeping you in my prayers.*

There are no magic words to express sympathy. Acknowledge the loss, and depending on your relationship with the parent or couple, a card of concern or flowers will be appreciated.

What Not to Say: *We never heard from you regarding the date or details of the visitation, memorial service, and/or celebration of life, so we didn't think we were invited.*

Really? Unless the service is private, a visitation, memorial service, or celebration of life is not an all-out party, and a personal invitation is never needed. When a death occurs, the grieving family is not only deeply mourning but most likely completely distraught and overwhelmed with planning final arrangements. All the to-dos following a death feel endless, and the ongoing tasks seem to never cease. Understand that the family may be emotionally exhausted and may not have had an opportunity to contact everyone with the specifics of the funeral arrangements. In fact, it's selfish to feel left out if you are unaware of the funeral particulars as it's easy to find out the details; do not put an extra burden on those mourning.

Instead: Take it upon yourself to ascertain the particulars. If you are close to the survivor or know the family or friends well and have not been informed of the specifics, text or call them to inquire about any arrangements. The conversation should be short and sweet to determine the important details. It's easy to search the internet for the city's newspaper and locate an obituary that most likely will highlight the funeral details. With a little effort and a bit of research, a lot of information can be found on the internet.

What Not to Say: *I'm sorry I won't be at the service(s); I don't do funerals.*

This statement is hurtful and one that a grieving family will not forget. It's not about you and that you *don't do funerals*; it's about the immediate family who are mourning a loved one. If you cannot provide the essential support because you *don't do funerals* (presumably due to feeling uncomfortable or awkward), then you should probably not attend the gatherings.

Instead: *I am unable to attend the service(s); please know you and your family are in my thoughts and prayers.*

For whatever reason you *don't do funerals*, it may be best not to offer an explanation.

What Not to Say: *I won't be able to attend the service(s) as I have a family reunion that day, and it's the only time my entire family will be together.*

This statement may break the hearts of those who just lost someone and whose family gatherings will never be the same.

Instead: *I am unable to attend the service(s); please know you and your family are in my thoughts and prayers.*

It's best not to offer an explanation if you prioritize attending a family reunion over showing support to those who experienced a loss. Be sensitive. Perhaps you can make a brief appearance at one of the funeral events and then slip away to attend the family reunion.

What Not to Say: *I won't be able to attend the service(s) as that's the same day as my work's holiday party.*

This statement shows priority to attend a holiday gathering over supporting a family or friend following the death of their loved one.

Instead: *I am unable to attend the service(s); please know you and your family are in my thoughts and prayers.*

If you choose a holiday party over attending funeral service(s) to comfort those grieving, it's best not to offer an explanation. Perhaps you can leave one event early to attend the other.

What Not to Say: *How are you doing?*

Gee . . . my loved one just died. . . . How do you think I'm doing? This statement shows genuine concern, and I am sure the person asking may not know what else to say. It's not about how uneasy you feel; it's about the person or family with ongoing hurdles in the healing process. Be prepared for someone to share dark and heavy emotions. You may be told more unsettling details than you are comfortable hearing or knowing.

Instead: *I've been thinking about you and your family. I can only imagine how difficult this time is for you; please know I'm thinking about you and your family.*

By acknowledging the trying circumstance or loss, you're expressing empathy. An alternative is to say, *How are you doing today?* or *How are you doing this week*? Putting the emphasis on *today* or *this week* makes this question a little more acceptable, and it opens the door for further conversation should those affected wish to expand. Recognize that some may not want to discuss and/or relive their sorrowful time. Be sensitive.

What Not to Say: *You are doing so well.*

Someone may look and appear to be doing all right following a devastating period, but realize he or she may be barely hanging by a frayed emotional spool of thread ready to unravel at any moment. Do not assume their emotional state.

Instead: *You continue to be in my thoughts and prayers.*

Acknowledge the painful time with heartfelt words of compassion.

What Not to Say: *You are so strong. I don't know how you got through that awful time. I couldn't have done what you did.*

These comments are a reminder of the tumultuous period

someone went through and may continue to endure. Those in crisis have no option but to face and deal with what is on his or her plate. It is not about you and whether you could have dealt with a similar situation.

For my children and me, I do not know how we lived through our horrendous ordeal either. I am just thankful that we got through the day without collapsing from painful emotional and physical turmoil.
Instead: *I'm heavyhearted for all you went through; you continue to be in my thoughts and prayers.*

Nothing more needs to be said. Acknowledge the trying time with heartfelt compassion.

What Not to Say: *Nothing.*

If you were aware of someone who went through a dark stretch, acknowledge that you have been thinking about him or her during the stormy period. Stop thinking about how uneasy you may feel; consider those who went through a trying time.

People I have known for many years have never acknowledged in any way what my family and I went through. I am absolutely baffled when I see them, and they act like it's just another day, people I considered friends. I do believe they care, and I can only assume they are hesitant about bringing it up. Perhaps they are apprehensive to say anything for fear of making me sad or upset or saying the wrong thing. Yes, I might tear up, but saying nothing is more painful and hurtful. As I said earlier, my husband did not stub his toe or have the flu—he died of a terminal illness. Being the sole caregiver for him for twenty-four hours a day for six months and being totally homebound for nine weeks of those six months was heartbreaking, overwhelming, stressful, and extremely emotionally and physically difficult.
Instead: *I have been thinking about you and your family.*

This statement is all that needs to be said. You acknowledge the hardship or loss and express genuine concern. A hug or gentle touch on the arm or shoulder shows empathy.

What Not to Say: *Give me a call if there is anything I can do for you.*

The person making this statement is genuinely concerned and has good intentions, but it puts unneeded pressure on the recipient to respond. They might not know what help is needed or have the time or energy to pick up the phone and ask for assistance.

Instead: *I don't know what to do to help you, but I am here to listen and support you.*

Those on the outside need to contact the ones in crisis, not the other way around. Be truthful if you want to lend assistance but may be unsure how to proceed; your honesty will be appreciated, and the recipient may be more comfortable calling on you.

What Not to Say: *I am sorry I have not touched base with you. . . . I have been so busy.*

There is no way anyone has been busier than those who have struggled with a major crisis. Being *busy* does not give anyone a free pass to lose touch or not offer support.

Instead: Touch base with those hurting, often; I cannot emphasize this enough. Again, it is not about you and your full calendar. No one wants to hear a lame excuse for being too busy to reach out. If you are a family member, close friend, coworker, neighbor, fellow church member, etc., you should be in touch on a regular basis.

What Not to Say: *I'm sorry I haven't been in touch; I thought you wanted some time alone.*

How do you know someone wants to be left alone? Unless specifically stated, do not assume anyone wants to be holed up. The time during and after a tragic period or death is when people need support from family, friends, neighbors, etc., more than ever.

Instead: It speaks volumes when you call someone just to touch base and check in. If you are only able to leave a voice message, state that you are thinking about them, which will mean a lot and may illuminate a somber day if the person is lonely, disconnected, or feeling forgotten. There is no excuse to disappear.

What Not to Say: *I know just how you feel.*

No—you don't. Everyone grieves in their own way.

Soon after John died, I said to a dear friend, "I'm not the first woman to lose a husband, and I am determined not to wallow in sorrow or throw myself a pity party." My friend replied, "But Tish, *you* have never lost a husband." After giving her words some thought, I realized she was right. I was entitled to low points. . . . *I* had never lost a husband. This was a life-changing event, and I had never experienced anything more devastating.

Instead: *I can only imagine how you may be feeling.*

Most people can *imagine* how it may feel to have gone through a similar situation, and this statement opens the door for further conversation should those affected wish to share.

What Not to Say: *I know just how you feel; it felt like a death when I went through my divorce.*

No—you don't. No one should compare a divorce to the death of a loved one. A divorce is the end of a relationship and emotionally devastating, but it is a different type of closure.

John and I were happily married. We did not choose to end our relationship as husband and wife; he died of a terminal illness. Death is final. I will never talk to or see John ever again.

Instead: *I can only imagine how you may be feeling.*

Most people can imagine how difficult it may be to lose someone special. Nothing more needs to be said; this statement shows empathy and compassion.

What Not to Say: *I know how you feel. When my pet died, I went through a long period of grief.*

No—you don't. The loss of a loved one cannot be compared to the death of a pet. Grieving a beloved pet is heartbreaking, and no one should trivialize the loss, yet equating a pet to a person is unfair.

Instead: *I can only imagine how you may be feeling.*

Nothing more needs to be said; this statement shows empathy and compassion. Be sensitive to someone's loss.

What Not to Say: *God only gives you what you can handle.*

What? Even though the intention of this statement may be sincere, the remark may deflate those trying to work through what occurred. Everyone has their beliefs, religious or not, and even those spiritually devoted may be wrestling with their faith following any crisis.

As a spiritual person, I do not believe God only gives someone what he or she can handle. I cannot believe someone would think the statement offers any hint of comfort.

Instead: *I can only imagine how difficult this time has been for you and your family.*

Nothing more needs to be said; this statement acknowledges the painful period and shows concern and empathy.

What Not to Say: *This was God's plan.*

What? Although the intent is to be positive, the remark is thoughtless, does not show compassion, and is not uplifting. Perhaps those who are highly religious feel that God plays a major role in all life events, but others may not be as spiritually devout. Anyone going through a trying ordeal may be struggling with his or her faith while attempting to process what occurred.

Did God plan for my family to endure our tragedy?

Instead: *You continue to be in my thoughts and prayers.*

This wording is thoughtful and caring.

What Not to Say: *He's in a better place.*

And what place would that be? Heaven? You may think this statement offers comfort, especially if someone suffered a tragedy or illness, but the survivors may be searching for hope and restoration, grappling with their faith, or attempting to sustain their beliefs. Anyone would prefer their loved one be among the living.

Instead: *I know you are hurting because of _____'s death.*

Nothing more needs to be said. This statement shows compassion and empathy.

What Not to Say: *Well, at least they are no longer suffering.*

The statement may be true, and the intentions honorable, but it is not comforting to those mourning the loss of a loved one.

Instead: *You and your family continue to be in my thoughts and prayers. I can only imagine how hard this time is for you.*

Both statements are sincere expressions of empathy and compassion.

What Not to Say: *Everything happens for a reason.*

Do you think this is healing, positive, or uplifting? This statement can be emotionally prickly. Most likely, those enduring a crisis are struggling to make sense of their trauma.

Instead: *I can only imagine how difficult things have been for you.*

You acknowledge the difficult time, and this statement shows sympathy.

What Not to Say: *Things will get better.*

This statement is intended to be encouraging, but realize there may not be a resolution in sight, and the winding paths may prevail for quite some time. Never downplay another's pain.

Instead: *You remain in my thoughts and prayers.*

Be sensitive; show compassion.

What Not to Say: *I heard you went through a difficult time. Why didn't you reach out to me? I would have brought you a meal, picked up something you needed at the grocery store, etc.*

These words are selfish attempts, perhaps not intentionally, to avoid guilt for not reaching out. Try not to burden the ones in crisis with self-centered comments.

Instead: If you were aware that someone had gone through a tumultuous period, *you* need to reach out to the ones in crisis, not the other way around. There is no excuse for remaining silent.

What Not to Say: *You need to (or should) put this behind you.*

No one should tell someone how to feel, process, deal with, or mourn the death of someone special. A painful trauma cannot be put on the back burner. Those hurting are trying to cope with their troubling emotions and attempting to heal; the unsettling feelings and unfortunate period will remain with them for the rest of their lives. Difficult situations may lessen as time goes on, but the above remark is not comforting.

Instead: *I continue to keep you in my thoughts and prayers; I'm here for you if you want to talk.*

Often, someone just needs the compassionate, nonjudgmental ears of others to unload feelings or voice worries. Can you find five to ten minutes in your day to listen to someone's concerns? Can you offer a trusting sounding board?

What Not to Say: *I cannot believe _____ passed away. I do not know how I'm going to go on without them.*

When speaking with a survivor, do not be so lost in your own sorrow that you fail to console the immediate family members or friends. It's not about you and how you are going to cope following a death; it's about the survivors who have lost someone special. Yes, others are mourning too, but the ones closest to the deceased should not be ladened with outside grief. Support and compassion

are needed the most, not sorrowful comments from others.
Instead: *I'm saddened by your loss.*

Keep it simple. The statement shows empathy and compassion.

What Not to Say: *How old was your loved one? Well, they lived a long life.*

A loss is a loss; age makes no distinction. The deceased was someone's spouse, partner, sibling, aunt, uncle, cousin, parent, grandparent, friend, neighbor, coworker, etc. Be sensitive to death regardless of age.

Instead: *I'm heartbroken for your loss.*

This statement is all that needs to be conveyed.

What Not to Say: *We need to get together . . . yet never calls.*

Do not expect those hurting to call you. You need to reach out to those grieving, not the other way around. Those affected are most likely experiencing many up and down days, and outsiders should be mindful of the roller-coaster emotions.

I cannot tell you the number of people who have said that we need to get together for lunch, dinner, or a gathering . . . and I have yet to hear from them even years later.

Instead: It's so simple. If you mentioned getting together, pick up the phone, call the affected person, and put a date on the calendar to meet. They will appreciate you reaching out.

What Not to Say: *I miss seeing you.*

This is a very common yet superficial statement. If you miss seeing someone, pick up the phone and touch base. Do not wait until a crisis is over to connect.

Instead: Pick up the phone and touch base during and after a stormy time.

What Not to Say: *I'm sorry I haven't called. I'm really bad at staying in touch with people.*

There is no justifying not reaching out or connecting with someone following a troubling situation or a death.

Instead: Take a few minutes to pick up the phone and touch base. Reaching out means a lot, is truly appreciated, and is heartwarming. It only takes five or ten minutes to connect. Your call just might be the highlight of someone's melancholy day.

What Not to Say: *Are you ready to come back to the committee (or class, club, group, etc.)?*

Really? Hmm . . . you never reached out to those affected during their distressing ordeal or following a death, and you want to know if the person is ready to return to the group? Is this an organization those hurting even want to return to?

Instead: *We've been thinking about you, and we would love to have you return to the committee (or class, club, group, etc.) when you are ready.*

Support should be ongoing from the start and continue when the hardship ends. Do not wait six months, a year, or longer to reach out.

What Not to Say: *It's been a year since that horrific ordeal, and she's still having a hard time.*

It's been a year since _____ died, and Susie is still really struggling.

Do not assume anyone is emotionally all right following a crisis. The emotional pain may be minimal or massive, but it truly never goes away.

Instead: Be sympathetic to someone's hardship or loss. There are no tried-and-true guidelines to navigate tragic events or grief. Reach out with empathy and compassion.

What Not to Say: *I'm sure you will find someone else.*

Following a separation, divorce, or death, the speaker may have had encouraging intentions, yet the one involved may find this statement uncomfortable and awkward and, frankly, in poor taste. Heartache and grief have no timeline, and the one hurting may or may not have any interest in dating, let alone even considering a future relationship.
Instead: Avoid the above remark. Emotions and ideals are individual and personal.

What Not to Do: *Disappear.*

Once a crisis ends, continue to reach out to those affected. When people are front and center during a turbulent ordeal and suddenly disappear when the hardship is over, those involved often feel let down and confused by the sudden silence.
Instead: Continue to reach out to those who have experienced a distressing period. Caring for those in the aftermath of a rough period should be maintained for a long time. Pick up the phone and continue to reach out following a crisis.

What Not to Do: *Send a text or email of sympathy.*

Sending a text or email of sympathy is thoughtless and impolite; there is no excuse for this behavior.
Instead: It's fitting to initially acknowledge a loss through a text or email, following up with a handwritten card. Sending a sympathy note through the mail is always appropriate, as is picking up the phone to express your condolences. Take the time to write a note of sympathy or touch base with those who experienced a loss. Calling those grieving opens the door for them to unload their feelings or concerns, and they will feel less alone as they mourn. It only takes a few minutes to convey condolences, and it's comforting to receive a note or hear words of sympathy.

What Not to Do: *Brush off attending a funeral visitation, memorial service, celebration of life gathering, or other planned end-of-life event honoring the deceased.*

There is no question that end-of-life gatherings are difficult and heavy. I am aware of a young man in his late twenties who was asked if he attended the services of his long-time close friend; I was told he shrugged his shoulders, replying, "No." The person asking continued, "Gosh. Why not?" The young man replied, "I don't know; I just didn't go." Hearing this exchange made me feel incredibly sad for the parents of the deceased, who most likely wondered why their son's close friend and possibly others failed to attend the service(s). Perhaps this young man felt awkward, uncomfortable, or was in such deep grief that he could not pull himself together to show up to the planned gathering(s).

Instead: Attend any events that are set if you are able. A visitation, memorial service, celebration of life, or other end-of-life gathering is a time to console the family and close friends who are mourning a tremendous loss. As hard as it is to sometimes do things that may feel uneasy and tense, your appearance at a funeral service(s) means a lot to the immediate family; they will appreciate and remember your presence.

What Not to Do: *Avoid the person or family having gone through a crisis or loss.*

Make a point to speak to those hurting. Yes, you may feel apprehensive or uneasy, and you might not know what to say, which is certainly natural. However, it is not about you and your hesitancy; it is about those who endured a heartbreaking period.

Many times, it was obvious when people I have known for many years have avoided my children and me. They saw us in passing or from afar, turned, and went in the opposite direction; it is very hurtful. Since my husband's death in 2015, I have yet to be approached by many people I have known for over twenty-five years who have never acknowledged my loss in any way. Some of these people I considered friends, and a few were an important part of my life in the last twenty-five-plus years, as well as in the lives of my children as they were growing up. Clearly, I thought more of the relationship than they did. If someone has failed to acknowledge my loss thus far, it would be very odd for them to say something now, many years later.

Instead: Approach and speak to those who have gone through a difficult time regardless of the nature of the circumstance. *I've been thinking of you and/or your family* is really all that needs to be conveyed. Most people find tremendous comfort when someone reaches out with a phone call to touch base or approaches them in person and acknowledges the painful time they went through.

What Not to Do: *Pick up the lunch/dinner tab.*

It is very kind and thoughtful to treat someone to lunch or dinner, but realize this can be a sensitive area for those who endured hardship. This gesture may put the recipient in an awkward position. Those affected may not want to feel indebted to their friend or may feel uncomfortable getting together in the future. Perhaps a one-time offer can be extended as a caring gesture. Be mindful of the circumstances and use your judgment to avoid uneasy situations.

Instead: In some cases, asking for separate checks may be a better option.

What Not to Say: *Where are you living now? When are you moving?*

These are very nosy questions. Why is it assumed that the widower, widow, partner, or family has moved or is planning to relocate?

Instead: Be sensitive.

What Not to Say: *I see you are still wearing your wedding rings.*

Wearing a wedding band following the death of a spouse or partner is personal and private and should not be questioned or judged. Personally, not only are the rings a reminder of the love I had for my husband, but my engagement and wedding rings have been a part of me for almost thirty-five years; I would feel lost without them.
Instead: Be sensitive.

Life is full of surprises, obstacles, and uncertainties and can be complicated and troublesome. Some people sail through life on top of the world, while others face challenge after challenge. No one is immune to a battle or tragedy; no one knows what is around the corner. Shouldn't we all try to lessen another's heartaches and burdens by offering comfort and support through empathy, compassion, and simple acts of kindness? We all have special gifts—providing a meal, running errands, sitting with an ill person, picking up the phone to touch base, driving someone to a doctor's appointment or therapy session, walking the dog, babysitting, undertaking yard work, doing laundry, housekeeping, etc. As you move on with your life, do not ignore or abandon those who are struggling.

                    Tomorrow is not a given.

                    Reach out.

Quick Guide on Ways to Reach Out

- Pick up the phone and touch base.
- Send an email to check in.
- Drop off or mail a card of concern/thinking-of-you note.
- Deliver fresh flowers, house plants, seasonal plants, or cheerful balloons.
- Offer to set up an online site so a family can update others on the situation and/or their needs.
- Organize a meal team/meal train.
- Organize a Fill the Freezer opportunity.
- Drop off a meal, freezer items, or other foods (soup, muffins, fruit, etc.).
- Grocery shop.
- Drop off a bagful of fresh fruit, snacks, or bottled water.
- Drop off paper products (paper towels, napkins, plates, cups, foil, plastic wrap, tissues, toilet paper, etc.)
- Deliver a gift card for groceries, books, and gas, to a restaurant, a big-box store, etc.
- Share extra servings from a meal (soup, casserole, salad, home-baked cookies, etc.)
- Offer to complete errands (banking, laundry, dry cleaner, purchasing stamps, mailing packages, pet items, etc.)
- Give cash for parking lot fees, valet services, hospital cafeteria, fast-food restaurant, gas, etc.
- Visit those suffering or hurting.
- Wash and dry laundry.
- Offer light housekeeping (vacuum, dust, etc.).

- Walk the dog.
- Water outdoor plants.
- Babysit; walk the children to/from the bus stop; offer to take the children to activities.
- Mow the grass, put out mulch, rake leaves, or shovel snow.
- Take the trash can/recycling bin to the street and return it to the house.
- Offer to accompany someone to a doctor's appointment, therapy session, medical treatment, attorney's office, court appointments, etc.
- Accompany someone to a funeral home, cemetery, or house of worship when planning end-of-life events.
- Offer to sit with someone in a hospital or home setting.
- Put together a gift bag or basket.
- Assist with insurance, medical paperwork, or bills.
- Help navigate technology issues.
- Assist in household tasks (bringing boxes up to or down from the attic, rearranging furniture, dropping off donations, taking items to the dump, etc.).
- Write thank-you notes for meals, flowers, gifts, memorial contributions, emotional support, etc.
- Take a car in for routine maintenance or automotive issues.
- Shop for upcoming birthdays or holidays.
- Lend any medical equipment or devices you are not using.
- Offer to help go through the deceased's clothes and personal effects.

Important Takeaways

- No one knows what someone else is facing, going through, or has endured.
- Everyone has a story, a personal journey.
- No one should ever feel alone, isolated, or forgotten during a troublesome time or the aftermath.
- No one should ever suffer in silence.
- Put yourself in someone else's shoes; what would help you if you were in their situation?
- Everyone needs support from others when enduring a difficult situation or following a painful ordeal or death.
- Acknowledge and address the tumultuous time.
- The focus of any conversation should be on those who endured a troubling period.
- Respect the need for privacy or boundaries specified.
- Realize there may be nothing you can say or do to make someone feel better or change things, but acknowledging the trying time and offering comfort and support means a lot.
- It's not about you; it's about the person and/or family dealing with a troubling time or loss.
- It's at difficult times when you know who your true friends are.
- Cards! Cards! Cards!
- Step outside of yourself.
- You or someone close to you will be on the receiving end of a hardship at some point.
- Show empathy and compassion through acts of kindness.
- Lend a helping hand.
- Everyone has a gift. What is yours?
- Reach out.

Acknowledgements

While discussing *Reach Out* with others, I have been asked several times, "What do you believe John would think of you writing this book?" I find this question interesting, knowing that if John had not had brain cancer and passed away, I probably would not have written this guide. Writing a book was never in my mind. I cannot begin to guess what John would have thought about turning our heartbreaking time into a resource for others, but I believe he would consider *Reach Out* an important endeavor. Reaching out to others is a topic that fuels me, and it is a rewarding feeling when I have done something helpful for someone else amid a troubling time.

Thank you, LauraBess Kenny, for editing the first two drafts. She inspired me to pursue this guide with her insightful comments and suggestions, helping me dig deep into my thoughts and feelings. She opened my eyes and soul to the world of writing.

Thank you, Koehler Books, for hearing my voice and passion on reaching out to others in crisis and backing me as a first-time author. The Koehler team helped make my dream a reality.

I cannot even begin to thank my family and friends who were by my side during a heartbreaking and challenging time and the aftermath. They held me up many days, sat quietly, and listened as I unloaded emotional baggage. I have told them how grateful I am, but saying it just doesn't seem like enough. I could not have gotten through the most heartbreaking time in my life without their friendship and kindness.

Finally, a special thank-you to Daniel, Alyssa, and Kevin for their continued encouragement and support while writing this book; this resource is their story too. Our troubling period has brought us closer and made us see life much clearer. It's people and the relationships we have with them that are important.

Reach out.

Bibliography

Cleveland Clinic. "The 5 Stages of Grief After a Loss." Cleveland Clinic Mental Health. March 21, 2022. https://health.clevelandclinic.org/5-stages-of-grief/.

www.ingramcontent.com/pod-product-compliance
Lightning Source LLC
LaVergne TN
LVHW091542070526
838199LV00002B/169